The Department Chairperson's Role in Enhancing College

Ann F. Lucas, *Editor*
Farleigh Dickenson University

NEW DIRECTIONS FOR TEACHING AND LEARNING
ROBERT E. YOUNG, *Editor-in-Chief*
University of Wisconsin

Number 37, Spring 1989

Paperback sourcebooks in
The Jossey-Bass Higher Education Series

Jossey-Bass Inc., Publishers
San Francisco • London

Ann F. Lucas (ed.).
The Department Chairperson's Role in Enhancing College Teaching.
New Directions for Teaching and Learning, no. 37.
San Francisco: Jossey-Bass, 1989.

New Directions for Teaching and Learning
Robert E. Young, *Editor-in-Chief*

New Directions for Teaching and Learning is published quarterly
by Jossey-Bass Inc., Publishers, 350 Sansome Street, San Francisco,
California, 94104. Second-class postage rates paid at San Francisco,
California, and at additional mailing offices. POSTMASTER: Send
address changes to *New Directions for Teaching and Learning,*
Jossey-Bass Inc., Publishers, 350 Sansome Street, San Francisco,
California 94104.

Editorial correspondence should be sent to the Editor-in-Chief,
Robert E. Young, Dean, University of Wisconsin Center, Fox Valley,
1478 Midway Rd., Menasha, Wisconsin 54952.

Library of Congress Catalog Card Number LC 87-644763

International Standard Serial Number ISSN 0271-0633

International Standard Book Number ISBN 1-55542-878-9

Cover art by WILLI BAUM

Manufactured in the United States of America. Printed on acid-free paper.

Ordering Information

The paperback sourcebooks listed below are published quarterly and can be ordered either by subscription or single copy.

Subscriptions cost $52.00 per year for institutions, agencies, and libraries. Individuals can subscribe at the special rate of $39.00 per year *if payment is by personal check.* (Note that the full rate of $52.00 applies if payment is by institutional check, even if the subscription is designated for an individual.) Standing orders are accepted.

Single copies are available at $12.95 when payment accompanies order. (California, New Jersey, New York, and Washington, D.C., residents please include appropriate sales tax.) For billed orders, cost per copy is $12.95 plus postage and handling.

Substantial discounts are offered to organizations and individuals wishing to purchase bulk quantities of Jossey-Bass sourcebooks. Please inquire.

Please note that these prices are for the calendar year 1989 and are subject to change without notice. Also, some titles may be out of print and therefore not available for sale.

To ensure correct and prompt delivery, all orders must give either the *name of an individual* or an *official purchase order number.* Please submit your order as follows:

Subscriptions: specify series and year subscription is to begin.
Single Copies: specify sourcebook code (such as, TL1) and first two words of title.

Mail orders for United States and Possessions, Latin America, Canada, Japan, Australia, and New Zealand to:
  Jossey-Bass Inc., Publishers
  350 Sansome Street
  San Francisco, California 94104

Mail orders for all other parts of the world to:
  Jossey-Bass Limited
  28 Banner Street
  London EC1Y 8QE

New Directions for Teaching and Learning Series
Robert E. Young, *Editor-in-Chief*

Contents

Editor's Notes

The quality of the undergraduate experience has come under increasing public scrutiny during the past few years. Enhancing the quality of teaching has become the central concern of professional organizations of higher education. Nevertheless, faculty members in higher education are experiencing conflict. While colleges and universities repeatedly intone the value of high-quality teaching, emphasis on research and publication is increasing. It was not surprising, therefore, when the Council of Independent Colleges reported that faculty morale seems to be highest in colleges where teaching is greatly valued, a clear sense of mission exists, faculty feel they have a meaningful role in governance, and scholarship (rather than research and publication) is rewarded (Rice and Austin, 1987).

The improvement of instruction has become the primary focus of faculty development offices. Sophisticated, knowledgeable staffs have created a variety of programs to improve the teaching-learning process, yet the impact of these offices on the total faculty has often not been very large. Faculty members, comfortable in the ways they have been teaching, feel they have no time to spend analyzing and improving their teaching when tenure, promotions, or salary increases depend more on research and publication. Others, convinced that they are doing an adequate job, see no reason to participate in sessions on teaching sponsored by faculty development offices.

Nevertheless, instruction in American higher education needs attention. Individual faculty members require support, encouragement, and sometimes direction. The curriculum needs reshaping, and the learning-teaching environment itself needs conscious nurturing.

In this volume, we argue that the academic department and the department chairperson are the key agents for maintaining and enhancing the quality of undergraduate education. Further, we contend that those chairpersons with the best knowledge and best resources related to college teaching and learning will be the most effective agents. This sourcebook has been designed to offer some of these resources in one volume.

What role does the chairperson play in sustaining and improving the quality of the undergraduate experience? How does the chairperson play that role? What resources does he or she need?

The first and last chapters of this book address the chairperson as instructional leader of the academic department and provide some practical concepts about that role and strategies for how to play the role.

1

All the chapters are written so that they can be useful to chairpersons from a wide range of settings and backgrounds.

Chapter One makes a distinction between the chairperson as transformational leader, a challenging and exciting role, and the chairperson as manager, a dreary job that leads to burnout. How does the role of instructional developer fit into the multifaceted tasks of the job? How can chairpersons motivate faculty? What power do chairpersons already possess, and how can power and influence be increased? The first chapter addresses these questions and others: How can one improve overall teaching in the department? What are strategies for motivating the alienated, tenured faculty members? How can one deal with difficult colleagues? The last chapter discusses strategies for creating a climate that can make teaching a valued activity in the department.

While the volume begins and ends with practical strategies on how a chairperson as leader in the department can motivate and contribute to faculty as teachers, other chapters describe additional approaches to instructional development. How chairpersons can develop a mentoring system for helping faculty to help their students learn is described in Chapter Eight. The use of student evaluations as feedback instruments to enhance professional development of faculty is the subject of Chapter Nine. For institutions that use teaching assistants, Chapter Seven provides a first-rate analysis of what they are normally hired to do and how we can train them to do it better.

Teaching strategies with the potential for drastically changing the essential nature of what goes on in college classrooms are covered in Chapters Two through Five. Department chairpersons, subjected to pressures that fragment their lives, find it difficult to keep current in their own disciplines as they try to cope with institutional demands. To go beyond one's discipline and become informed—for example, about how to analyze and improve the effectiveness of lectures, get students to become more actively involved in learning, increase participation through problem-based learning, use one's discipline to teach critical thinking, and increase learning for adult part-time students—requires large time commitments usually unavailable to chairpersons.

In this volume, instead of a literature search in the field of instructional development in higher education, a chairperson may find within reach at the corner of the desk a single source of practical information and workable strategies that can be shared in a variety of ways to enhance teaching in the department. Each chapter has been written by individuals—teaching faculty members, faculty development specialists, and department chairpersons—who understand departments and the special role of the department chairperson. Although the authors are all people who have written about the topic before, these chapters have been written specifically with the needs of department chairpersons in mind.

Ann F. Lucas
Editor

Reference

Rice, E., and Austin, A. *Community, Commitment, and Congruence: A Different Kind of Excellence. A Preliminary Report on the Future of the Academic Workplace in Liberal Arts Colleges.* Washington, D.C.: Council of Independent Colleges, 1987.

Ann F. Lucas is professor and chairperson of the Department of Management and Marketing at the Teaneck Campus of Fairleigh Dickinson University, where she is former chairperson of the Psychology Department and founder and former director of the Office of Professional and Organizational Development.

*A department chairperson who is a transformational leader
creates a shared commitment to the quality of college
teaching.*

Motivating Faculty to Improve the Quality of Teaching

Ann F. Lucas

The task of chairing an academic department is one of the most difficult
and challenging positions in higher education. The complexity of a
department chairperson's work is increased by a role that demands that a
chairperson be both faculty member and administrator. The increasing
organizational emphasis on accountability causes a chairperson to feel
more and more like an administrator, a concept alien to many chosen to
be chairpersons. In institutions where there is collective bargaining, the
problem is compounded by whether chairpersons are in or out of the
bargaining unit; yet for chairpersons to forget even for a moment their
status as faculty members places them in jeopardy with members of their
departments.

Adding to the challenge and the complexity of a chairperson's
work is its importance to the institution. Because the faculty's primary
ties in a college are with the department (or division), departmental
leadership is an essential determinant of faculty morale, which is the
greatest single factor affecting the quality of students' undergraduate
experience. At the same time, chairpersons are overworked and often find
themselves bogged down in a numbing routine of paperwork and

A. F. Lucas (ed.). *The Department Chairperson's Role in Enhancing College Teaching.*
New Directions for Teaching and Learning, no. 37. San Francisco: Jossey-Bass, Spring 1989.

managerial activities. Becoming physically and psychically drained contributes to a loss of perspective on the leadership role that a chairperson can perform.

In any given week, an academic department chairperson may be called on to make decisions concerning a bewildering variety of managerial issues usually unrelated to his or her specialized area of competence. A chairperson may be called on to decide whether a section should be dropped because of low enrollment, or to wait another few days to see whether the class minimum size is achieved; to attend or conduct a college, committee, faculty, or department chairpersons' meeting; to listen to and help resolve student problems; to interview a promising applicant to temporarily replace a professor who may or may not return after surgery; to finish preparing for and teach a class; to be an advocate for faculty needs; to handle a large volume of paperwork; to attend a special campus event; to listen to and see what can be done about faculty members' complaints that classrooms are too hot, too cold, too noisy, or that needed supplies are running low; to find someone who is willing to represent the department at a parent weekend or student open house sponsored by admissions; to negotiate for the department with the dean; to help find a faculty speaker for a student club or community organization; to respond to a request from public relations, the office of development, or the alumni association; to speak on behalf of the department to the business office, the bookstore, library services, instructional media, or physical plant maintenance; and to deal with yet another incident in a long-term feud between two faculty members.

While these responsibilities, in conjunction with the demands of one's own teaching or research, can often constitute a formidable obstacle to regular eating and sleeping habits, they are not a chairperson's most important job. Chairpersons must also find time to be leaders.

A distinction between a manager and a leader is that a manager focuses primarily on maintaining the status quo, while a leader inspires others to a shared vision, thus empowering them so that extraordinary things can be achieved in an organization. A leader is a role model who shows what can be done by example, an individual who recognizes individual contributions and celebrates accomplishments (Kouzes and Posner, 1987). When one is functioning as a leader, there is an excitement about being a department chairperson; when one functions as a manager, the job is dreary and uninspiring.

In a survey administered during workshops I have conducted during the past three years, almost a thousand department chairpersons were asked, "What would it take to make yours a high-quality department?" Three of the five responses elicited most frequently are all related to faculty motivation: (1) improve the quality of teaching in the department, (2) develop faculty commitment to departmental goals, and

(3) increase scholarship and/or research and publication. In this same survey, department chairpersons were asked to indicate on a five-point scale how successful they had been in dealing with a number of faculty development problems. About three-fifths of them indicated that they were unsuccessful or very unsuccessful in at least one of the following important areas: improving the overall teaching effectiveness in the department, improving the quality of performance of those who are poor teachers, motivating alienated tenured faculty, and motivating burned-out faculty members. In this chapter, each of these issues will be addressed, and some recommendations will be made that can be adapted creatively to your own individual leadership style and situation.

Motivating Faculty Members

One of the most difficult tasks for many chairpersons is that of motivating faculty. One oft-repeated question—"How do you motivate faculty, particularly the tenured, alienated faculty, when you have neither carrots nor sticks?"—reflects the feeling of powerlessness more prevalent in higher education than in other organizations. The system in which chairpersons are appointed by deans, but only after being elected by colleagues or after consultation with department members, or simply by rotation, convinces many chairpersons to avoid any action that might be unpopular or that might suggest a chairperson is assuming any more power than one is entitled to among peers. Thus, chairpersons conclude that they have no power in their departments.

Sources of a Chairperson's Power

Chairpersons do have power, though, power that they can increase and use to achieve important goals. *Power* is not used here in a manipulative or exploitative sense; rather, it is defined as the ability to influence others to engage in activities that improve the quality of education. Power derives from two sources: position and personal influence. Position power comes with the title; it is a mantle of prestige and authority associated with the position. As chairperson, one speaks on behalf of the department, has significant input into personnel and sabbatical decisions, requests and allocates resources for the department, and has final authority over faculty schedules. A chairperson can pass on information about paid consulting jobs, assist faculty in networking with other professionals, and create opportunities for faculty visibility and professional development both inside and outside the organization.

Personal power, by contrast, must be earned. Most faculty will make a commitment to a chairperson whom they respect and perceive as honest and fair in dealing with others. Personal power also derives from having respect and standing in the discipline and the institution, from interpersonal effectiveness and a knowledge of how to get things accomplished within the organization, from access to information about certain administrative plans and decisions, and from overall perceived credibility with administration and faculty (Tucker, 1984).

Important tools for increasing one's power as a chairperson are fairness, honesty, and consistency. Credibility with the dean can be established by doing your homework before attending meetings (know the agenda and understand the topic) and by being logical and rational in your opinions, recommendations, and decisions.

Chairpersons' credibility with faculty can also be enhanced by approaching problems in a positive, rational fashion instead of in a negative, emotional one. The way a chairperson presents an issue influences faculty's willingness to resolve the problem. For example, the dean requests that the department offer some classes during the early morning and late afternoon hours. From the faculty point of view, these are not very desirable time slots. The chairperson can present this information to the faculty by saying, "The dean has thrown the schedule back at us again, with a complaint that we cannot all teach our classes between ten and two," or the chairperson can say, "With the way classes are currently scheduled, students have difficulty taking the courses they need in our department. Let's talk about how we can deal with this problem in a way that is fair to everybody." The way a problem is identified frequently determines the solutions that are generated.

Transformational Leadership

In addition, chairpersons can develop personal influence and commitment from colleagues and move toward transformational leadership—a style characterized by an ability to motivate people to achieve extraordinary things (Bass, 1985)—by recognizing contributions, using positive reinforcement, and celebrating accomplishments. Faculty members often say, "You get very little thanks around here for anything you do. People want things done yesterday, but nobody seems to appreciate the extra effort you make for them." Colleges and universities are bureaucratic institutions where individual excellence often elicits little in terms of reinforcement. Because chairpersons have regular contact with their faculty on a day-to-day basis, they are in the best position to provide that appreciation and acknowledgment.

When it comes to transformational leadership, chairpersons have bottom desk drawers full of fifty-dollar bills, and the supply is inexhaustible—even though we distribute large numbers of them, the drawer is always full. Reinforcing faculty for achievements and contributions doesn't require that a chairperson have a large budget. Although a simple private or public "thank you" to an individual or a group is always welcome, a letter from the chairperson means even more. A covered-dish supper at home to celebrate the accomplishments of faculty members who have received academic promotions or special awards or had books or papers published may require some effort, but it is an effective way to strengthen faculty motivation and establish an understanding of what is valued in the department.

Sometimes faculty members also feel that their units are not well known or highly regarded in the college. On a regular basis, a chairperson should request information from faculty about their accomplishments, which can then be submitted for publication in college newsletters, alumni magazines, and the local and national press.

Leaders, particularly transformational leaders, serve departments in which faculty members feel an excitement about being part of an important enterprise, where they are encouraged to take risks and are supported if they fail, where people know they make a difference. Chairpersons do have power, a great deal of power, to motivate faculty and achieve the important goals of the department.

Special Techniques for Improving the Quality of Teaching

How, then, can we motivate faculty to improve the overall quality of teaching in the department? First, we can work at becoming transformational leaders instead of simply managers of departments. This means challenging a system that says chairpersons cannot motivate faculty because chairpersons have no power. Recognizing that power is both legitimate and necessary, we accept what position power we have and do our best to earn personal power. We develop a shared vision of a department in which faculty and students participate in creating a high-quality undergraduate experience. How do we get started?

Faculty members in almost every department would agree that they place a high value on teaching, but when was the last time we discussed it in the department? When did we last share with one another information about a class that went really well? When did we last ask a colleague for advice on how best to present a difficult concept? Does the topic ever come up at a department meeting?

Taking Risks

Since the subject of what goes on in the classroom seems to be a very private one in many colleges, how does a chairperson introduce the topic of teaching effectiveness in the department? Being a transformational leader requires that one take risks and be willing to fail. Obviously, not everything we try will work. One of the task functions of leadership is to initiate the structure to make something happen. A chairperson has the power to set the agenda for department meetings. (Of course, once a preliminary agenda is developed, a chairperson also asks for additional agenda items from faculty.) A chairperson can place instructional development on the agenda.

When this agenda item is reached at a meeting, how does a chairperson handle the topic? Although everyone has a personal style, you might say something like "I placed this item on the agenda because I've been reading about some recent innovations in college teaching, things like how one can get students more actively involved in the classroom, how to lead good discussions, and how to teach critical thinking. It occurs to me that we haven't talked about teaching in a long time, and yet we all value good teaching. I was wondering if two or three of you would be willing to do a workshop for the rest of us on some of the teaching strategies you have tried that really worked in getting students more involved in class." Wait long enough for a few people to volunteer. If you do not get any volunteers, choose one: "Jim, I've heard students talk about some of the small-group work (or experiential learning, or role plays, or case studies) you have used in your classes. Would you be willing to share that approach with us? Who else would be willing to do this?" Since there are currently so few occasions provided for us to talk about our successes, chances are you will soon have your workshop presenters. During this department meeting, determine the date and time of the workshop, indicating your firm expectation that every member of the department will attend because teaching is an issue that is central to enhancing the quality of the undergraduate experience.

Depending on the politics in your organization, you might ask your faculty members how they feel about inviting the dean to such a workshop. On the positive side, his or her attendance emphasizes the value placed on teaching in your college. On the negative side, faculty are less likely to discuss problems they have had in teaching if the dean is present—unless, of course, the dean is willing to talk about an occasional problem or two he or she has had in the classroom. If faculty agree that the dean should be invited, discuss your goals with the dean ahead of time. Indicate that supportive, reinforcing behavior characterized by openness would create a very desirable role model.

Be certain that the minutes of the department meeting include the discussion and plans for a workshop on teaching. Write simple notes thanking those who volunteered to be presenters. As the date for the workshop approaches, send out a memo reminding the faculty of this event, and do it with enthusiasm. Think through what role you will play in the workshop. Will you introduce the discussion, chair a panel, take an active part in the discussion of teaching strategies that follows the formal presentation, or simply thank the presenters at the end of the workshop? Whatever you choose to do, be certain to ask what kind of follow-up faculty members want, and line up a topic and presenters for another workshop that same semester. Chances are that people will find such a discussion stimulating and informative and will see it as an opportunity to open up issues related to the whole teaching process.

Faculty usually respond well to discussions about teaching, since there are currently so few opportunities to discuss this activity, which is central to their lives. Probably most people will also come away with one or two strategies they would like to try in their own classes. Feel free to suggest other topics for workshops. Some that explore significant issues are:

- What makes a lecture good?
- What are some alternatives to lecturing?
- How can we involve students more actively in learning?
- What are useful strategies for leading a good discussion?
- How can our discipline be used to teach critical thinking?
- How does a student's level of cognitive development affect what he or she can learn, and what are the implications for teaching?
- What are departmental expectations for student performance?
- How can examinations be constructed so that they reflect the goals of the course?
- What are some factors related to increasing student retention? (Hint: Use early, frequent feedback and opportunities for bonding.)
- How can classroom management issues (for example, students who dominate discussions or who are disruptive or shy) be handled?
- How do we prevent cheating and plagiarism?
- How can we communicate clear expectations to students?

Included in the volume you are reading are chapters about many of these topics, written by individuals who are well informed about current issues.

After a workshop has been held, thank the faculty presenters by writing each a special note, placing a copy in their personnel files, and forwarding a copy to the dean. Once again, this is recognition that is valued but not often received in academe.

Motivating Tenured Faculty Members

What motivates faculty? Faculty members are clearly among the most intelligent members of our society. All were highly motivated to pass through the hurdles involved in completing a graduate degree, particularly a Ph.D., and advance in rank within the institution. What has happened to some of our tenured faculty members? How can we motivate them again?

In my survey, motivating faculty members is the faculty development task at which department chairpersons most frequently feel they have been unsuccessful. Most of us came into higher education with a dream. That dream may have focused on being part of a community of scholars from whom we would receive intellectual stimulation and emotional support in our discipline. Perhaps we felt we would do that definitive research study and share our findings with others, or the dream may have emphasized passing the torch on to the next generation of scholars. We may have dreamed that students would listen attentively to every word we said and be inspired by us, but once we joined a college or university, we began—slowly for some, quickly for others—to separate the realities of academia from the dream with which we started. Some of us may have started with unrealistic expectations and were thus doomed to disappointment.

Most faculty are experts in their disciplines but have never learned how to teach. Edgerton (1988) underscores this problem: "Faculty members come to us strong in content and blissfully ignorant of anything having to do with theories of learning and strategies of teaching rooted in pedagogical knowledge. In their knowledge of their disciplines . . . they stand on the shoulders of giants; in their knowledge of teaching, they stand on the ground" (p. B2).

A new faculty member walks into a classroom for the first time with a role model of a favorite professor in mind and uses those teaching strategies that he or she most admires. Before too many semesters pass, some new faculty will discover that they are experiencing little satisfaction in teaching. Moreover, it is humiliating to admit they are having problems reaching their students. Since everyone in the department seems to take for granted that the Ph.D. prepares one for the demands of teaching, there seems to be nowhere to turn for help. Years go by, and rationalizations develop to protect self-esteem: "Although I am well qualified and an excellent teacher, students these days are not intelligent enough, not well motivated, or don't have the skills to benefit from what I have to offer."

Other faculty become alienated later on. After they have held places of esteem in their departments, there comes a time when their opinions and advice seem to be ignored; or after occupying positions of prestige, they see others assume the leadership roles in a department. Because this hurts, faculty members may show by their behavior that they are displeased. They may make it very clear that they are not committed to an activity that many others in the department are enthusiastic about. As time goes on, their displeasure is felt by other members of the department, and they begin to be ignored. They and their colleagues are now adversaries. The perception on both sides is that it is too late to do anything about alienated faculty members. The alienated may look for some outside work—sometimes prestigious consulting activities, but often something mundane like painting apartments, opening a motorcycle shop, or acquiring some kind of business. Engaging in such activities often has symbolic value: "If I am not appreciated by those donkeys in my department, I can at least do other things to increase my income or help me gain some satisfaction."

How can a department chairperson motivate such an alienated faculty member? A successful approach often involves something as simple as demonstrating some human caring. There are people in some departments who have not said more than "hello" to another member of the department for years. A chairperson can make a point of greeting such a faculty member warmly, ask how things are going, discuss some topic of general or academic interest, ask an opinion or advice about something, even occasionally invite him or her to lunch.

At some point, one might say, "You haven't been to a department meeting in a long time. I remember when I used to look forward to hearing your point of view on issues we discussed. What keeps you away these days?" If this question releases a tirade, do not try to correct his or her perceptions. Do some active listening and nonjudgmental summarizing of what you hear. When some of the emotion is spent and the bitterness is aired, you might say, "I think I have a better understanding of how you feel, but we'd really like to have you back as part of the team." No agreement may be reached on that occasion, but you will have other opportunities, and he or she will have time to think about what you have said. Another approach is to ask an alienated faculty member to attend a meeting to give a report on a relevant topic, one that you know he or she is knowledgeable about. Be sure to express appreciation. If you know an area in which he or she has some particular expertise, find a way of using this knowledge in the department. Often an alienated faculty member would like to find a way back into the mainstream but may be too proud or concerned about possible rejection to try to do it alone.

Orienting New Faculty Members

When we realize how difficult it is to reverse the process of alienation, prevention starts to look very attractive. It makes good sense to allocate resources to orienting and socializing new faculty members to the requirements of academe. (One of the most useful ways to accomplish this is through the mentoring system proposed in Chapter Eight.) A new faculty member might even be paired up with an alienated faculty member who has good teaching skills. Such an arrangement can be a mark of respect and a way of sharing the expertise of the alienated individual with a new faculty member. There are certainly risks, but some of them can be reduced through careful individual preparation of both parties to the mentoring arrangement.

Working with Burned-Out Faculty Members

For faculty members who have been teaching the same courses (particularly introductory or service courses) and taking the same committee assignments for a number of years, life can become repetitious and dull. Professional growth and change are the most useful prescriptions for such individuals—a challenging assignment, a new course, a different responsibility, or a new activity. Tucker (1984, pp. 127–130) lists dozens of possibilities. Introducing such changes might best be done after discussing with the individual his or her goals for professional development and what might be most interesting and satisfying. A mentorship arrangement with a new faculty member might help an individual to look at classes with the excitement of a new perspective.

The transformational model of leadership suggests that when department goals are met by also achieving individual goals, motivation is greatest. What are faculty members' goals? Faculty are most likely to be motivated when they feel that they are part of an important ongoing enterprise—when they feel that they make a difference. We can all remember a time when we worked eighty hours a week because we felt that something we were doing was important and that we were making a significant contribution to something we believed in. It also helped if we felt someone else appreciated what we were contributing. This is the task of the transformational leader.

Leadership is a challenge. We must see things as they might be. We must fashion a vision of our future. We must inspire others by sharing this vision and empower them to realize it. We must make our departments places where people can share a sense of excitement and know they make a difference. This is what distinguishes a leader from a manager. As chairperson, we are in a singular position to make this happen. Will we serve out our terms defending the failure of the status quo, or will we strive to make a difference?

References

Bass, B. M. *Leadership and Performance Beyond Expectations.* New York: Free Press, 1985.

Edgerton, R. "Melange." *The Chronicle of Higher Education,* April 20, 1988, p. B2.

Kouzes, J. M., and Posner, B. Z. *The Leadership Challenge: How to Get Extraordinary Things Done in Organizations.* San Francisco: Jossey-Bass, 1987.

Tucker, A. *Chairing the Academic Department.* New York: Macmillan, 1984.

*Ann F. Lucas is professor and campus chairperson of the
Department of Management and Marketing at the Teaneck
Campus of Fairleigh Dickinson University, where she is
former chairperson of the Psychology Department and
founder and former director of the Office of Professional and
Organizational Development.*

How can the chairperson create a climate that supports instructional effectiveness?

The Lecture: Analyzing and Improving Its Effectiveness

L. Dee Fink

Lecturing is the most common form of teaching activity at the college and university level. It has survived the advent of the printing press as well as video and computer technology. Clearly, something about it is very attractive. Some scholars on college teaching, like Eble (1976), have argued that lecturing has persisted in part "because it is the easiest thing to do; it is the accepted thing; it is the safest." Despite the obvious omission from this list of the claim that it is the best form of teaching, Eble has also noted that lecturing nonetheless offers what books and television lack: "face-to-face confrontations with other talking, gesturing, thinking, feeling humans" (pp. 42–43). That is, lecturing offers a personal presence that has high value, even in classes with large numbers of students.

As chairpersons know so well, however, college professors vary quite widely in their lecturing abilities. Some are quite good. In their classrooms, the audience feels engaged, attentive, and energized. Others are not so good. When this happens, the mood of a classroom is quite different. Spread out over the course of a semester, these classes result in low attendance, poor results on exams, and low evaluation marks for teachers.

A. F. Lucas (ed.). *The Department Chairperson's Role in Enhancing College Teaching.*
New Directions for Teaching and Learning, no. 37. San Francisco: Jossey-Bass, Spring 1989.

Can teachers make significant improvement in their lectures? The answer to this question is clearly yes. As the instructional consultant on a moderately large campus, I have seen many faculty members make dramatic improvements in their teaching. But for chairpersons interested in raising the quality of teaching in their departments, the question is one of how to conceptualize the lecturing problem so that the most effective approach might be used to strengthen the good lecturers and assist the less successful ones. My classroom observations have led to a model of successful teaching that can be helpful to department chairpersons in assessing and improving lecture performance.

Characteristics of Lecturing

When I began to analyze the observations from my classroom visits, I noticed that different professors had different kinds of strengths, as well as different kinds of problems. Eventually, four kinds of differences emerged as significant. Some are fairly obvious and relatively easy to change; others are more subtle and more challenging to change.

Presentational Quality. Given the fact that most classes consist of lectures, the first feature that impresses an observer is the lecture's quality as a presentation. One major part of this is basically physical in nature. Is the teacher projecting his or her voice adequately? Does the teacher move around or stay in one place? Is the voice a monotone, or is it modulated appropriately in pitch, loudness, and pacing? Does the teacher make appropriate use of facial expressions and body gestures, or is the body unexpressive? Does the teacher make eye contact with the students, or does he or she look at his notes or off into space?

A second part of the presentational quality of a lecture pertains to its intellectual character. Is the lecture clearly organized? Does the speaker have an interesting way of opening and closing the lecture? Are the examples well selected? Are the arguments well developed? Are different points of view taken into account? Are the explanations clear?

Presentational quality is what audiences are usually most conscious of. This is what students talk about after class, and questions about this show up frequently on course evaluation forms. This means that problems in this area often get relatively quick attention, even though they may be less fundamental than some other problems. This point does not mean that presentational problems are unimportant. An excellent idea poorly presented still has little educational value.

Appropriateness of Use. This characteristic involves the question of whether the teacher is relying excessively on the lecture as a teaching technique. When I visit a class, one of the things I note and categorize is the type of activity occurring: TT = teacher talk, TQ = teacher question, SA = student answer, SQ = student question, and TR = teacher response.

Some teachers appear to be "talkaholics"; that is, the only thing they seem to know how to do as teachers is talk. Their classes consist almost entirely of TT, fifty minutes at a time, forty-five times a semester, with time out only for midterm exams.

Other teachers realize that lectures can take many forms other than nonstop teacher talk: lecture-discussion, lecture-demonstration, lecture-recitation, lecture-laboratory, and so on. These other forms simply mean that from time to time the teacher stops lecturing, and something else happens in class. In addition, good teachers realize that for some courses, or for certain segments of a course, some more active form of teaching and learning is preferable to lecturing—for example, case-study discussions, small-group problem solving, or in-class writing activities.

Intellectual Stimulation. The third characteristic is considerably more challenging to deal with, but almost anyone who has sat through many lectures will know what I am referring to. Simply put, some lectures are intellectually alive and exciting, and others are not. Although many factors influence this characteristic, a key one is the speaker's view of knowledge: Does the teacher see knowledge as static or dynamic, as a product or a process?

The answers to these questions can usually be found in the way the teacher treats the subject. Does the lecture present a rhetoric of conclusions or a rhetoric of inquiry? Does the lecture constitute a description of knowledge or a quest for knowledge? Has the audience been presented with a question or a problem that it sees (or can be persuaded to see) as important?

Interpersonal Rapport. This final characteristic is also easily recognizable to listeners: Does the speaker succeed in making contact with the audience? Good speakers use a variety of techniques to achieve this effect: eye contact, humor, a dramatic problem, a poignant story, and so on. The effect is always there. The audience feels drawn in, close to the speaker, and hence ready to listen.

When the speaker does not succeed in making contact, the audience members feel a million miles away. Hence, their attention wanders, they watch the time, they do not ask questions (if such are solicited), and so forth.

This factor may seem similar to the preceding one, intellectual stimulation. The difference is this: The third factor is concerned with whether the content of the lecture is dynamic, the fourth factor pertains to the affective relationship between the speaker and the audience. Do listeners feel attracted to the public persona presented by the lecturer? Do they seem inclined to accept the lecturer as their instructional leader, either for the moment of the lecture or for the semester?

I would note that the four characteristics that I have observed function independently. A lecturer may rate high on appropriateness but low on intellectual dynamism, or one may be high on rapport but not well organized. A poor lecturer is someone who rates low on all four; a decent lecturer is one who does well on some but not on others; a superb lecturer is someone who is high on all four characteristics.

Four Dimensions of Teaching

After these observations, I felt the need for a model of teaching that would account for the differences among college teachers. Such a model could guide the assessment and improvement of teaching in general, but particularly lecture teaching.

The model illustrated by Figure 1 suggests that teaching can be described in terms of four dimensions: skills, decisions, philosophy, and attitudes. The shape of the diagram implies the relationship among the four dimensions. Teachers' attitudes about students and about themselves influence their philosophy of teaching and learning; this philosophy forms the context for their decisions about instructional strategies, which in turn determine which classroom skills are invoked and used. This means that, although skills are the most visible of the four dimensions, a teacher's philosophy and attitudes are the most fundamental.

Skills in Classroom Communication. Some faculty members, as a result of talent or prior experience, have developed reasonably good skills in classroom communication. They are reasonably competent in the physical skills as well as the intellectual skills of making effective presentations. Others are not so accomplished. They have not yet learned how to move around the room, vary their voices to emphasize key points,

Figure 1. Four Dimensions of Teaching

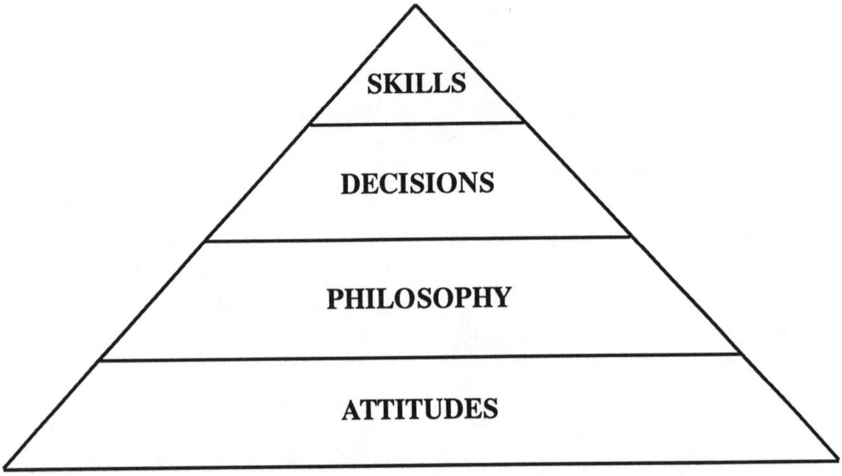

make gestures that liven up a lecture, create interesting openings to a lecture, develop clear summaries for the closures, and so on. As a result, even though they may have much to offer students, they are not fully effective as teachers.

Classroom communication skills, like all skills, are learnable with the right kind of coaching and the necessary effort to practice and hone these skills.

Decisions Concerning Instructional Strategies. Before we ever walk into the classroom, we have to make certain decisions about what we are going to do and what we want the students to do. For some college teachers, this task is fairly simple. They take their cues from the table of contents of the text and talk their way through the list of topics, adding their own examples or ideas as their intellectual resources allow. They want the students to listen and understand, take notes, and do the assigned homework.

Other teachers approach this task differently. Before they decide which teaching and learning activities would best suit a given course, they ask a number of situational and contextual questions: What do I want students to learn in this course: formulas, principles, problem-solving skills, an appreciation of the topic, or what? Do I need to spend some time at the beginning of the course to develop their interest, or are they already interested? How can I help them learn how to learn about this kind of subject matter? Does the department want this course to attract majors, cull out unqualified students, prepare students for a national exam, or what?

Only after answering such questions do they proceed to make decisions about instructional strategies: Will lecturing, or some other kind of classroom activity, best accomplish my instructional goals? If lecturing is appropriate, should it be complemented, either in class or out of class, by other activities? If experiential activities (for example, lab work, field work, demonstration, films) are called for, should these precede or follow the lectures?

Decisions about the choice of teaching and learning activities and the sequence of these activities determine the educational structure of a course, which in turn has a major impact on the effectiveness of the course.

Philosophy of Knowledge, Teaching, and Learning. In order to act as a teacher, one has to have certain beliefs and values about knowledge, teaching, and learning. Teaching is a goal-seeking behavior and, as such, it forces us to make choices about which goals are preferable (values) and how best to attain them (beliefs).

What is knowledge? Teaching? Learning? What is good knowledge? Good teaching? Good learning? Most of us could not quickly articulate our answers to these questions, because we have not thought about them or talked much with others about them. We would have to infer our answers from our behavior and the choices we make as teachers.

For example, do we view knowledge as a product or as a process? People who talk about teaching in terms of transmitting knowledge would seem to accept the "product" view: Knowledge is something that can be given by one person to another. Others would disagree, saying that knowledge cannot be given; it can only be created internally—by the learner.

Some people's view of teaching, if inferred from their classroom behavior, would seem to be "Teaching = Lecturing = Presenting Information." Most experts in the field of instructional development would consider this to be a very limited and limiting view of teaching. A broader definition of teaching might be something like "helping students learn." This, then, leads to a definition of learning.

"Listening to and understanding a lecture" might suffice as a definition of good learning in the minds of some teachers. Others have argued that listening to a lecture can do a reasonably good job of showing students what a teacher has learned about a topic, but ultimately students have to learn how to learn about the subject for themselves. This is the basic argument for including more active learning in a course: discussions, case studies, problem solving, role playing, collaborative learning, writing, and so forth. When this happens, however, the teacher's role changes drastically, from one of lecturing to one of creating learning tasks, providing feedback and encouragement, and coordinating learners who are moving at different rates or in different directions.

Attitudes Toward Students and Toward Oneself. Since teaching is by definition a social activity, one's attitudes toward students and toward oneself are important. We all have images of students: individual students, a class as a whole, actual students, and students in the abstract. Depending on these images, we also have feelings about them. We like them or we do not; we like this characteristic, but we do not like that one. To an extent, this affects how we behave toward students. Teachers with negative attidues toward students frequently have difficulty gaining the cooperation of students in the learning enterprise.

In the same vein, some professors seem to have difficulties as teachers because they are not able to see themselves as effective leaders in the classroom. Their self-images appear to be limited to that of knowers or doers and do not include a sense of what it would be like to be a teacher, an intellectual leader of others. We need to have realistic assessments of our own strengths and weaknesses, but we also have to have a vision of ourselves that we are capable of becoming, if we want to grow and develop as effective teachers.

Our images and feelings play a crucial role in our performance as teachers. If we believe that students can, they will; if we believe that we can, we will. As teachers, we need to have or to find images of ourselves and of our students that will facilitate interaction toward the common goal of learning.

Making Improvements

How can chairpersons best use this model to help faculty members in their departments improve their teaching? The first task is to determine which of the four previously described dimensions of teaching can produce the most significant improvements in faculty members' teaching: enhanced classroom skills, better decisions about teaching strategies, broader philosophies of teaching and learning, or more positive attitudes toward students or themselves. To decide this, information needs to be collected from a variety of sources and then analyzed with some care.

Basically, there are four sources that can be tapped in order to gather information about a faculty member's teaching: the teacher, a videotape or audiotape, students, or some third party (for example, a colleague or an instructional consultant). Most professors, while teaching, direct some portion of their attention to evaluating themselves, to assess how they are doing at the moment. This feedback is more immediate and more understandable to the teacher than any other source of information, but no one can catch everything that is happening in a classroom. Also, everyone has his or her own perceptual blinders. These are the limits of self-evaluation.

Videotapes and audiotapes do catch everything (or at least all sights and sounds). They can be very revealing, but recordings do not tell us, for example, whether our pace of delivery is too fast or too slow for students—that is, recordings of our teaching do not indicate the effects of our behavior. To get that information, we need to turn to the third source, our students. Their test performances and opinions tell us the effect of our teaching, but students are not skilled at analyzing why our teaching is having a particular effect. For that, we need a competent colleague or a specialist in analyzing classroom instruction. By visiting our classrooms in this unique role, they can make observations and connections that often would not occur either to the students or to the teacher.

Because each of these four sources of evaluation offers a unique kind of information and yet has an important limitation, a thorough evaluation requires the use of all four. Once a sufficient variety of information has been collected, it is time for some approach toward improvement. One approach is to identify the most significant problems and then try to determine which dimension is responsible. For example, if students feel they are not getting much out of a class, are the lectures not well organized, or has the teacher selected a teaching strategy that makes the students too passive? Was a limited teaching strategy chosen because of a limiting view of what constitutes good learning? Did the students sense that the teacher had a negative image of what students were capable of learning? Another approach is to analyze possible strengths to build on. Does the teacher have a certain attitude, philosophy, or classroom skill that could serve as the basis of designing a more effective teaching strategy?

Either approach requires two kinds of information: a detailed knowledge of what is occurring in a teacher's course, and a sense of what could occur. The former requires the thorough process of evaluation (already described); the latter may require the chairperson or the professor to enlarge his or her sense of the possible.

The rest of this chapter describes activities and readings that could be used to strengthen each of the dimensions of teaching, particularly as they relate to lecturing.

Classroom Skills. Video or audio recording can be the least obtrusive way to begin work on classroom skills and gives excellent information on the verbal content and exchange in a classroom. A videotape can help with body movements, facial expressions, and gestures. Used periodically, these recordings indicate whether skills are improving and whether the changes are the ones desired.

Useful readings on this topic include the ideas and language of the theater applied to making lectures in particular and teaching in general more dramatic and energetic (Timpson and Tobin, 1982; Kain, 1986). They consider writing the script (the content of lectures), using props (blackboard and demonstration devices) and costumes (dressing up or down for a particular audience), manipulating space effectively, and making an effective delivery.

People who rely primarily on lecturing as a teaching device make the quality of their teaching primarily dependent on the quality of their own performance. Therefore, any tips on how to improve performance skills should have high value.

Improving classroom skills, however, is not a one-time effort. Classroom skills, like all skills, need constant practice. Just as baseball players continually practice their hitting, throwing, and fielding, so do teachers find that they constantly need to work on voice delivery, body movement, and gestures.

Instructional Strategies. A good exercise to determine the nature of a teacher's current strategy is to audiotape one or two classes and then categorize what you hear when you play the tape, using the categories described earlier (TT, TQ, SQ, SA, and so forth). If most of the tape is TT, the teacher is relying heavily on the lecture mode of teaching, perhaps excessively so.

To help decide whether a teaching strategy is adequate or needs to be changed, try the following exercise. Make four vertical columns on an unruled sheet of paper, and label the columns *goals, evaluation, learning activities,* and *resources,* as shown in Figure 2. Then fill in each column for a given course, starting with the left-hand column. Under *goals,* you should list three to five goals for the course. Examples might include solving a certain kind of problem, designing a research project, writing a particular kind of essay, or analyzing problems from a certain perspective.

Next, under *evaluation,* you should briefly describe for each goal how you are going to evaluate students' learning. What would the students have to be able to do for you to know that the students had learned something? This will provide the basis of the evaluation design and the grading system for the course.

Next, for each goal, identify the *learning activities* that would allow most students to successfully complete the evaluation task defined in the second column. Typical activities might be analyzing problems, discussing issues, interpreting research data, writing creative or analytical essays, reading selected materials, and listening to speakers.

Finally, identify what *resources* are available to help students with the learning activities listed in the third column. These might be reading materials, technology, people, places, or things.

The point is to thoughtfully select an important set of learning goals and then, as you fill in the other columns, be sure that sufficient learning opportunities are provided for each goal.

Figure 2. Planning Sheet for a Course

GOALS	EVALUATION	LEARNING ACTIVITIES	RESOURCES
1.			
2.			
3.			
4.			
5.			

Several of the chapters in this book offer excellent suggestions for alternative instructional strategies, especially Chapters Three, Four, and Five. Previous issues in the New Directions for Teaching and Learning Series have also focused on different ways of teaching. Of special interest might be those on critical thinking (Young, 1980), writing (Griffin, 1982), small groups (Bouton and Garth, 1983), and problem solving (Stice, 1987). One other useful resource is Davis (1976), who has described four general kinds of teaching strategies that show a wide range of possibilities.

Since lecturing is so common, much has been written on how to plan and design effective lectures. Brown (1978) presents a series of activities to improve a person's ability to "unlock understanding" when lecturing. Bligh (1971) analyzes the value and limits of lectures. He also includes techniques for more effective lecturing, as well as alternatives to lecturing. Lowman (1984) summarizes the different forms and functions of a lecture. Frederick (1986) describes eight ways a lecture can be made more varied and lively, even in large classes. McKeachie (1986) summarizes research on the relative effectiveness of lecturing and offers tips on successful lecturing. Eble (1976) comments on "the lecture as discourse" with wit and style and presents a practical list of do's and don't's.

Philosophy of Knowledge, Teaching, and Learning. Modifying one's philosophy is considerably more challenging than, for example, increasing the frequency of one's hand gestures while lecturing, but it is ultimately more important and therefore worth the effort.

The key activities are reading, talking, and thinking about one's subject and how one learns and teaches it—first, to find out what one's philosophy is, and then to decide what it might be. This is where visits to the classes of other professors, followed by discussions, can be especially productive. What do they do that is different? Why do they do it? How do students react? Such questions will start the process of making explicit the assumptions a person has made unconsciously about what is true and what is good about teaching and learning.

A second technique would be to anwer the set of questions developed by Axelrod (1973, pp. 42-51). After interviewing numerous college professors, he observed that everyone has a teaching prototype— that is, an image of a good teacher. He also concluded that there are four basic prototypes, which are reflected in his short descriptions: "I teach what I know," "I teach what I am," "I train minds," and "I work with students as people." His analysis and list of questions work through issues raised by different views of teaching. He also presents the story of one professor, showing how a person's philosophy of teaching can change over time.

A large amount of literature exists on the subject of good teaching. Lowman (1984) presents his answer to the question of what constitutes masterful teaching. He has a model of effective teaching that I find appealing and very persuasive. Eble (1983) gives a mature reflection on the proper aims of teaching. Eble (1976) also presents ten "myths of teaching." Barzun (1945) and Highet (1950) represent classic statements on college teaching by two people highly regarded for their scholarly prowess. Epstein (1981) has assembled essays on sixteen memorable teachers as remembered by their former students who also became well known.

General critiques on higher education often address the philosophical dimension. These frequently look at the question of worthwhile knowledge and learning, rather than teaching per se, and hence frequently focus on curriculum issues. Recent publications, like Association of American Colleges (1985) and Bloom (1987), are important precisely because they challenge us to rethink our assumptions about the most worthwhile kinds of knowing and learning and offer us new possibilities to consider.

Attitudes Toward Students and Oneself. Perhaps even more challenging than changing one's philosophy is the task of reorienting one's attitude. Whatever attitudes we possess have resulted from many years of personal experience and hence are resistant to deliberate efforts to modify them. Nevertheless, people have made such changes, and the task is at least possible.

If we turn first to ways of relating better to students, the task seems in part to require new roles and different mechanisms for interacting with students—something other than a continuous pattern of "throwing your best in front of them" and then finding that "they don't appreciate it or don't get it." Different roles can lead to different responses and, given enough time, to different attitudes. The goal is to create better dialogue, in and out of class.

Many professors have explored ways of meeting with students in situations different from that of the regular classroom. Kogut (1984) borrowed the idea of quality circles from Japanese management techniques. The basic idea is to designate a group of students in the class who can meet with the professor out of class to talk about how the class is going and how it might be improved. Kogut used one group of students the whole semester. Another professor I know uses a different group of students each time, in order to get to know more students better. My own experience, and that of others who have tried this technique in whichever form, indicates that this not only improves the quality of decisions about instructional design but also has an impact on the attitudes of the teacher and of the whole class. They are in dialogue, communication occurs, and each side gets a renewed respect for the other.

Another professor with a large class has used the idea of having all students sign up for ten-minute office visits after the first exam. This is the only way students can find out their grades. If the students did well, the teacher uses this occasion to compliment them; if they did poorly, he tries to help them—for example, by discussing their study habits. In the process, he gets to know and understand the students better.

On our campus, we also had an opportunity for a group of fifteen or so faculty members to work on modifying their attitudes toward students. They gathered every two weeks for lunch and a one-hour meeting with different kinds of students: ethnic minorities, honors students, handicapped students, adult students, athletes, students from rural areas, and so forth. Each meeting pursued the question of what teachers could do to work most effectively with particular kinds of students. By the end of the year-long series of meetings, all participating faculty members felt enlightened and were willing to work closely with different kinds of students. The point is that structured dialogue, over time, was able to change faculty attitudes, given the willingness to change at the beginning.

Two kinds of reading material seem helpful for anyone wanting to understand students better. The first identifies different types of students. Mann and others (1970) conducted sophisticated research on the psychological meanings of different kinds of classroom behavior on the part of college students. They identified eight kinds of students, whom most faculty members will recognize. Lowman (1984) offers comments and tips on classroom dynamics and interpersonal skills. He also summarizes much of Mann's work and shows how it applies to the classroom. The second kind of reading material describes changes in students over time. Perry (1970) has developed a conceptual scheme for understanding the changes that occur in students during their college years. He describes the movement from dualism to relativism to informed commitment. Belenky, Clinchy, Goldberger, and Tarule (1986) offer a somewhat broader developmental scheme, which starts with reliance on received knowledge and moves to a discovery of subjective knowledge (listening to one's inner voice), procedural knowledge (reasoning), and eventually to constructed knowledge.

The task of changing one's attitude toward oneself is perhaps the most challenging of all. Because of this, significant change is most likely to come from something like an extended workshop or a multiday retreat aimed at personal change. Some universities are fortunate enough to have such resources on campus. On my campus, for example, the Office of Personnel Services periodically offers a seminar for faculty and staff that is designed to give people techniques and a conceptual framework for personal growth. A joint program at two other major universities uses retreats, informal peer groups, and growth contracts specifically to support the professional renewal of faculty (Povlacs and Hartung, in press).

As for readings, Mann and others (1970) identify and elaborate on the significance of six roles the teacher can fulfill in the classroom: expert, formal authority, socializing agent, facilitator, ego ideal, and person. Lowman (1984) specifically addresses two topics related to attitudes: the psychology of the teacher and classroom leadership.

Conclusions

I have tried to present a framework that can be used to analyze and assess both the lecture as a particular teaching technique and, more generally, teaching in whatever form it occurs. The benefit of recognizing the four dimensions of teaching and their relationship to one another is that anyone wanting to improve lecturing or teaching can use this scheme as a guide for assessing and improving practice.

A chairperson can facilitate this process by being aware of the different dimensions of teaching, taking time to assist faculty members in their departments in whatever ways seem most appropriate, offering encouragement for efforts to improve, and offering tangible rewards for improvements achieved.

Faculty members are ultimately responsible not just for being adequate or good but also for getting themselves on a growth curve, for continually searching for ways to improve themselves as teachers. This is where an understanding of the four dimensions of teaching can be especially helpful. Even though instructors may have developed competence in the skills necessary for one form of teaching (for example, lecturing), they may find a reason to change their attitudes or philosophies—prompted, perhaps, by new understanding of the value of teaching critical thinking. A change in these deeper dimensions will likely require consideration of new teaching strategies—for example, those involving more active learning—that may then demand competencies in a different set of classroom skills, such as designing and setting up small-group learning projects.

In sum, our goal is the long-term growth of the teaching faculty in a department, a goal that chairpersons and faculty members have reason to share.

References

Association of American Colleges. *Integrity in the College Curriculum: A Report to the College Community.* Washington, D.C.: Association of American Colleges, 1985.
Axelrod, J. *The University Teacher as Artist.* San Francisco: Jossey-Bass, 1973.
Barzun, J. *Teacher in America.* Boston: Little, Brown, 1945.
Belenky, M. F., Clinchy, B. M., Goldberger, M. R., and Tarule, J. M. *Women's*

Ways of Knowing: The Development of Self, Voice, and Mind. New York: Basic Books, 1986.

Bligh, D. A. *What's the Use of Lectures?* Devon, U.K.: D. A. and B. Bligh, Briar House, 1971.

Bloom, A. *The Closing of the American Mind.* New York: Simon & Schuster, 1987.

Bouton, C., and Garth, R. Y. (eds.). *Learning in Groups.* New Directions for Teaching and Learning, no. 14. San Francisco: Jossey-Bass, 1983.

Brown, G. *Lecturing and Explaining.* London: Methuen, 1978.

Davis, J. R. *Teaching Strategies for the College Classroom.* Boulder, Colo.: Westview Press, 1976.

Eble, K. E. *The Craft of Teaching: A Guide to Mastering the Professor's Art.* San Francisco: Jossey-Bass, 1976.

Eble, K. E. *The Aims of College Teaching.* San Francisco: Jossey-Bass, 1983.

Epstein, J. (ed.). *Masters: Portraits of Great Teachers.* New York: Basic Books, 1981.

Frederick, P. "The Lively Lecture—Eight Variations." *College Teaching,* 1986, *34* (2), 43–50.

Griffin, C. W. (ed.). *Teaching Writing in All Disciplines.* New Directions for Teaching and Learning, no. 12. San Francisco: Jossey-Bass, 1982.

Highet, G. *The Art of Teaching.* New York: Knopf, 1950.

Kain, E. "The Mass Class as Theatre—Suggestions for Improving the Chances of a Hit Production." In R. McGee (ed.), *Teaching the Mass Class.* Washington, D.C.: American Sociological Association, 1986.

Kogut, L. S. "Quality Circles: A Japanese Management Technique for the Classroom." *Improving College and University Teaching,* 1984, *32* (3), 123–127.

Lowman, J. *Mastering the Techniques of Teaching.* San Francisco: Jossey-Bass, 1984.

McKeachie, W. J. *Teaching Tips: A Guidebook for the Beginning College Teacher.* (8th ed.) Lexington, Mass.: D. C. Heath, 1986.

Mann, R. D., Arnold, S. M., Binder, J. L., Cytrynbaum, S., Newman, B. M., Ringwald, B. E., Ringwald, J. W., and Rosenwein, R. *The College Classroom: Conflict, Change, and Learning.* New York: Wiley, 1970.

Perry, W. G., Jr. *Forms of Intellectual and Ethical Development in the College Years.* New York: Holt, Rinehart & Winston, 1970.

Povlacs, J. T., and Hartung, T. E. "Integrating Individuals and Organizational Needs." In J. H. Schuster and D. W. Wheeler (eds.), *Enhancing Faculty Careers: Strategies for Renewal.* San Francisco: Jossey-Bass, in press.

Stice, J. E. (ed.). *Developing Critical Thinking and Problem-Solving Abilities.* New Directions for Teaching and Learning, no. 30. San Francisco: Jossey-Bass, 1987.

Timpson, W. M., and Tobin, D. N. *Teaching as Performing: A Guide for Energizing Your Public Presentation.* Englewood Cliffs, N.J.: Prentice-Hall, 1982.

Young, R. E. (ed.). *Fostering Critical Thinking.* New Directions for Teaching and Learning, no. 3. San Francisco: Jossey-Bass, 1980.

L. Dee Fink is director of the Instructional Development Program at the University of Oklahoma. He also teaches in the Department of Geography and serves as curriculum coordinator in the College of Liberal Studies.

Tell me, and I'll listen. Show me, and I'll understand.
Involve me, and I'll learn.

—Lakota Indian Saying

Involving Students More Actively in the Classroom

Peter J. Frederick

Imagine four different faculty members entering the department chairperson's office with the following concerns: "I know we're supposed to involve students more in the classroom, but I can't cover the material without lecturing. Besides, I have two hundred students, and I teach in an auditorium with fixed seats in tiered rows. Interaction is impossible." "My favorite professor in college always lectured, and I loved it! A lot of students today do, too; they're not paying money to hear other students exchange their ignorance and prejudices, which is all a discussion is." "You know, I've been trying some discussions, and even some of that small-group stuff, but it doesn't work. They're never prepared, and I usually end up lecturing anyway." "I'm getting tired of my own voice. I like discussions and would like to involve students more in the classroom, but I don't know how."

These scenarios raise fundamental issues not easily resolved. Problems of student passivity, lack of motivation, and attrition result from too little involvement of students in their own learning. Student involvement is achieved in many ways: trying out ideas in a discussion, participating in a small-group or role-playing exercise, practicing a skill, writing a paragraph or solving a quantitative problem, or even listening

A. F. Lucas (ed.). *The Department Chairperson's Role in Enhancing College Teaching.*
New Directions for Teaching and Learning, no. 37. San Francisco: Jossey-Bass, Spring 1989.

to a lecture or looking at a slide. There are also many ways to be an effective teacher.

This chapter addresses two ways in which chairpersons can encourage more active learning. The first is for faculty to make use of ten fundamental principles of teaching and learning intended to defuse the defensiveness evident in the comments of the first two professors. Second, department chairpersons can describe practical strategies for involving students more actively in the classroom, each of which is adaptable to any size class in any kind of room.

Fundamental Principles

There is no better list of fundamental principles than the "Seven Principles for Good Practice in Undergraduate Education," based on numerous studies and forged at a recent Wingspread conference of leaders in higher education (Chickering and Gamson, 1987). Each of the seven can serve as a beginning for thinking, talking, and acting to improve the teaching in a department.

Active Learning. Ask the members of your department to recall and describe "their best day" as a teacher or a particular classroom session when student motivation and learning seemed to be high. Invariably, they will talk about a day when the professor's role was diminished and there was a great deal of student energy and involvement, often around some issue that connected their world and values with the particular content of the course that day.

Respect for Diversity. Since different students learn in different ways and are at different levels of cognitive and affective development, diverse teaching styles and strategies are essential. Different students are both challenged and supported by each new approach. Diversity, moreover, means respecting the multicultural perspectives present in most classrooms. If the teacher does not structure interactive experiences, then black and white students, men and women, and older and younger students cannot learn from one another's experiences.

Cooperative Learning. Student learning is enhanced when challenged by diverse views and supported by collaboration with others. Learning groups and peer tutoring are powerfully effective ways of responding to the problem of students with different ability levels in the same class.

High Expectations. As the Wingspread report notes, expect more and you will get it. Self-fulfilling prophecies happen all the time in teaching, and we want to fulfill positive rather than negative prophecies. Students, like us, need to have their feelings acknowledged, so tell them, "I know it's a difficult assignment, but don't be discouraged. Hang in there and you can do it," and they will perform far better than if we criticize them for not being as well prepared or motivated as we once were.

Feedback. Students learn better and are more highly motivated when they receive frequent feedback on how well they are doing—by quiz results, comments on short writing assignments, reactions to points raised in discussions, and especially by personal expressions of support and by respect for their ideas and concerns. We need feedback from them, too, and not just at the end of the semester on some quantitative, universitywide form. Try Cross's (1987) idea of "minute papers" at the end of several classes throughout a term. Ask students, in one or two minutes, to write the most significant thing they learned today and the question uppermost in their minds at the end of class, in order to get a quick profile of the class and how well students are understanding the material.

Practice. Students learn by doing, by practicing and applying what they are learning, and by getting quick feedback on their efforts. They need, as the recent research suggests, "time on task." This means practicing skills in class as well as out.

Student-Faculty Contact. All of the principles cited thus far depend on a close, interactive relationship, not only among students but also between each of the students and caring, creative, enthusiastic teachers who empower their students to be the best they can be.

To these seven principles, I would add three more, intended to encourage our effort to adopt more active learning strategies.

Energy Shifts and Spaces for Student Ownership. The distinction between lecturing and discussion is troublesome. Depending on our goals, we need to use many different methods of instruction, not only from day to day but also within one class period. Learning theorists—and our own rather universally sad experience—suggest that after twenty minutes a student's ability to focus attention and retain learning drops off. Therefore, we need to think of class periods in terms of twenty-minute blocks; at the end of each block there should be a shift in which student energy is recharged by a change in activity. For example, after a minilecture on a new concept or theory, ask students to write on a specific application or synthesis question and then, perhaps, to pair off and explain their thinking to other students. After about fifteen to twenty minutes of writing ("practice") and pairs ("cooperative learning"), the energy shifts again, and the final ten to fifteen minutes of class are spent on discussing student responses. On the basis of this ("feedback"), the professor provides closure to the lesson. Students have participated in that outcome ("active learning") and now have a stake in the learning themselves. This variety of pedagogical approaches (a minilecture, writing, small groups, and discussion) can be achieved in any classroom—around a seminar table or in an auditorium, with twenty or two hundred students.

Visual Reinforcements. Like it or not, we are teaching students raised not just on TV but on MTV. We must recognize the important role visual reinforcements play in learning. This means not only putting lecture outlines on the blackboard or on an overhead projector but also using more slides, transparencies, maps, diagrams, visual images, handouts, and written summaries to reinforce verbal content. The larger the class, the more need for visuals, but learning in discussions is also aided by a visual summary of major points.

Appropriate Strategy. There is no more important moment in a professor's planning than when he or she says explicitly, "Given my general goals for this course and my particular goals for this unit, and given what I am learning about these students and myself, the appropriate teaching strategy for next Wednesday is X." Thinking about goals and selecting a strategy has a lot to do with the coverage issue. There is no good answer to the first professor's concern about coverage except to acknowledge that, yes, active learning strategies do indeed mean we will cover less content, but what we gain instead is heightened motivation and the development of more critical thinking. If students do not hear as much from the professor (notice I do not say *learn*), they get more practice in how to learn for themselves. It is a trade-off. How we choose to teach depends on our goals.

Strategies

This section briefly describes ten strategies for active learning that a chairperson can share with, or even demonstrate to, department members.

The Oral Essay. Since, as Fong (1987) reminds us, the silent student is not necessarily an uninvolved student, a traditional lecture executed with the kind of excellence to which we all aspire—and once in a while achieve—is the first active learning strategy. Lectures are valuable in imparting new information, explaining and classifying difficult concepts, modeling an active creative mind solving a problem or challenging old habits of thinking, inspiring a reverence for learning, and motivating enthusiasm for further study. The oral essay is a polished work, which skillfully makes only two or three points around a single intellectual question or problem. It has unity: The topic is introduced, illustrated with several concrete examples, and concluded within fifty but preferably twenty to thirty minutes. An outline, and perhaps some slides or transparencies, serve as visual reinforcements as the students listen in awe to the professor's "perfect" presentation.

Using Pairs and Writing to Energize Students. When we ask students at the end of an oral essay if there are any questions, there usually are not, for the obvious reason that we have already said it all. What if we followed a thirty-minute lecture with a focused question or task, to be done in writing or talked about with another student in pairs or trios?

We face a similar situation when starting the discussion of some text with a variation of the question "How did you like it?" Silence. Students, potentially eager to participate, suddenly discover something on their desks that requires their full concentration. Rephrasing the question sometimes helps, as does being able to wait out the silence. The problem is not necessarily the question, nor is it that students have not done the reading. Rather, most learners need time and space to absorb a question before they can respond to it.

After suggesting the crucial question or questions for a discussion, ask students to do one of two things: "Take out a piece of paper and spend two or three minutes writing down your thoughts," or "Pair off with the person next to you and take just a couple of minutes to discuss the question together and how you might respond." After either one of these very brief exercises, or perhaps both, repeat the question. The students are energized, and there will be several ready to participate. The reasons are obvious. Students have been given space and time to incorporate the question into their reading, experience, or other preparation for class and to practice their responses, either on paper or with another student. In short, they own the learning; they now have an investment in their ideas and are ready to risk them. This strategy is especially helpful for reticent students, and it slows down the quicker, competitive ones, who often dominate discussions.

Brainstorming. Brainstorming is another useful strategy for getting quick feedback from many students on how well they understand a new topic or concept. Begin class by inviting them to call out everything they know or think you know about American Indians (or Brazil, Marxism, market economics, Hemingway, particle physics, the Renaissance, or whatever) or to explore the multiple meanings of key words. Ask students to call out as many definitions as they can for romanticism (or culture or feminism). A list will unfold of a mixture of specific facts and events, impressionistic feelings and prejudices, and even intepretive judgments. Students bring to most courses both some prior knowledge and considerable misinformation. Since anything goes in brainstorming, students feel free to participate, and faculty members find out quickly what students already know and do not know.

The only rule of brainstorming is to acknowledge every offering by writing it down, thus providing a visual record and honoring student contributions. As ideas are proposed, teachers might arrange them in rough categories. Alternatively, ask students to suggest groups and patterns and to comment on the accuracy and relative importance of the array of facts, impressions, and interpretations. Refinements can be dealt with by erasures, a luxury not allowed in the formal lecture. When the class is over, an organized configuration of the ideas contributed by students and instructor will appear on a transparency or chalkboard. This evolving visual set of ideas, which students have helped create, reinforces their learning and engages them actively, no matter the class size or room.

Concrete Images. Since contemporary students are visual learners, it is obvious that active learning is facilitated when focused on the concrete. To begin a class with description (*who, what, when,* and *where* questions) will later help students engage in higher-level analysis and evaluation (*why* and *why important* questions). Begin, therefore, by asking students to state one concrete image that stands out from a text, scene, event, laboratory experiment, or art object: "From your reading of *The Color Purple* (or *Candide,* or a management case study, or whatever), what one specific scene or moment stands out?" As students report, the collective images are listed on the board and provide a visual record of descriptive recollections as a backdrop to the analytical discussion that follows. As in brainstorming, the recall of concrete scenes prompts further recollections, and a flood of images flows from the students. As a follow-up question, invite the class to study the items on the board, and ask, "What themes or patterns jump out at you? What connects these images? Is there a pattern to our recollected events? What is missing?" A variation is to show one slide or overhead transparency filled with images and interpretive possibilities and ask students first to describe what they see and then to consider abstract questions of meaning and value. In both cases, with texts or visuals, facts precede analysis; the concrete leads to the abstract. Furthermore, many students (all of them, if seated around a table in a smaller class) get to participate actively, and the discussion has a clear and common central focus.

Using Questions and Small Groups. The use of questions is, of course, at the core of active learning. We all know how to ask the recitation question, for which there is a correct answer. More difficult is to get the class involved in open-ended or problem-solving questions. Pairs and writing are a helpful way to begin, as are small groups.

No matter the size of a class, it can always be broken down into smaller groups of two to six students. Small groups will work well in responding to a question, to the extent that instructions to the groups are clear, simple, and task-oriented. "Which person in the *Iliad* best represents the qualities of a Greek hero?" "Agree on what you think is the crucial turning point in Malcolm X's life." "Decide together what Van Gogh's painting says to you." Be certain directions are clear: "Take about twenty minutes, and be sure to select someone to keep notes and report back to the larger group when we come back together at 10:30." A plenary closing session is crucial in small groups.

So far, we have looked at questions we ask, but students also have their questions, and they can learn to formulate better ones. There are many ways of generating questions. To ask students ahead of time to prepare one or two questions about their reading, or an issue, will increase the likelihood that they will come to class prepared to discuss. To ask a question that hooks the content to their issues guarantees it even more.

A good way to conclude a unit is to invite students to finish the following sentence: "A question I still have about the Holocaust (or slavery, or Kant, or India, or enzymes, or the New Deal, or reality therapy, or whatever) but have been afraid to ask is . . ." This is a good exercise, both for giving students an opportunity to clarify their learning and for giving the professor some feedback on how well a particular unit or concept has been learned. The students should be asked to write their questions on cards and either bring them to class or turn them in early. Both ways help reticent students get their questions asked. Questions on cards can be given either to the professor or to a student to read.

Another variation (less favorable to reticents) is to ask students, as they arrive for class, to call out questions about the text or topic they hope will be answered that day. Listed on the board, the questions provide an agenda. Interventions are necessary, both in the middle and at the end of a discussion, to ask, "Where are we?" or "What are the three most important points we have explored or settled so far?" or "What one or two questions are still unresolved?" In large classes, it may be necessary halfway through a period to divide students into small groups and ask them to take five minutes to agree on one crucial question. Seeking group consensus sorts out more thoughtful questions and leads to some peer teaching and learning, as students answer one another's concerns in quest of a consensus. The plenary closure session provides the professor with feedback and students with a reassuring sense that their questions are shared by others.

Problem Solving. The problem-solving class begins with a question, a paradox, or a compellingly unfinished human story—some tantalizing problem that hooks student interest. "What brought the two former friends, one in blue and one in gray, to oppose each other on Cemetery Ridge in Gettysburg that hot July afternoon?" In this example, the implied problem—an open one—is "What caused the Civil War?" Resolving an issue (depending on what it is or in what field) may require a scientific demonstration, a mathematical proof, an economic model, the outcome of the novel's plot, or a historical narrative. Problem solving is an ideal way of shifting energy back and forth between teacher and students. The problem is first presented in lecture, inviting students to fill in imaginative spaces in the story with their own unfolding solutions as they listen. The process becomes overtly interactive when the professor elicits the students' tentative solutions to a problem or completions of a story, lists them on the board, and initiates a discussion. "What do you think will happen? Which solution, outcome, or explanation makes the most sense to you?" If there is no consensus, the teacher lectures a little more, invites a new set of student responses, and asks the question again.

Reading and Other Skills of Critical Thinking. Students today, we are told, do not know how to read or think. If so, there is no more important active learning strategy than an old-fashioned technique: *explication du texte.* Students can develop their thinking skills through practice in closely reading and analyzing passages together in class. Any number of students, following along in their books or handouts or on an overhead projection, can first observe a professor working through selected passages of a document, speech, essay, poem, proof, or fictional passage, and then practice it themselves. On reaching a particularly ambiguous passage, small groups of three to five students can be asked to decide what they think the main point is (shifting the energy), or invite students to select their own quotations, which they think are particularly important, and to say why. Lively involvement is guaranteed, because students will not select the same quotations or interpret a passage the same way. The professor's response to different group reports provides feedback and furthers learning.

This process for critical thinking can be used for other than just verbal texts. Art historians, musicologists, economists, and anthropologists have traditionally shown students how to "read" an abstract painting, sonata, supply-and-demand curve, or artifact. Natural scientists explain their "texts" with elaborate demonstrations (and labs for practice). Social scientists train students in other analytical skills— quantitative analysis of graphs, charts, and tables and the use of maps, interview schedules, or census and polling data. In sum, whether you use verbal texts or quantitative data, make sure students have a copy of the document in question, and then follow three steps: modeling by the professor, practice by the students, and feedback.

Debates. For instructors uncomfortable with the uncertainty and potential lack of control implicit in decentralized classes, the debate offers both widespread student involvement and firm professorial control. Take advantage of the central aisle dividing large lecture halls (or two sides of a table) in order to structure a debate. Students can either support the side of an issue assigned to the half of the room where they happen to be sitting or, as prearranged, come to class prepared to take a seat on one particular side of a debate: "Burke or Paine?" "Evolution or creationism?" Put signs up labeling the two sides, and open the debate with a simple question: "Why are you sitting where you are?" Whichever approach a professor uses, he or she maintains rigorous control: "From the right side of the room, we will hear five arguments on behalf of intervention (in Nicaragua, the market), after which we will hear five arguments against from the left." Repeat the process once or twice, including rebuttals, before asking for two or three volunteers to make summary arguments for each side. Although neither one of two polar sides of an issue contains the whole truth, it is pedagogically energizing and valuable, if only to point out the complexity of truth, for students to be compelled to choose and then defend one side of a dichotomous question. When some students quite rightly refuse to choose one side or the other, create a middle ground and invite their reasons for choosing it.

Role Playing and Small Groups. For teachers occasionally willing to risk some emotion and classroom chaos, role playing is a powerful learning strategy with the potential to motivate, energize, and achieve widespread interaction among students. Role playing can be as simple as asking two members of the class to volunteer to act out an executive and an adviser trying to arrive at a difficult decision, or two scientists thinking out loud about the significance of an experiment, or two social workers handling a troublesome family crisis. Issues involving value conflicts, moral choices, and timeless human dilemmas related to the students' world usually work best, but role playing need not be so personal.

I have written elsewhere (Frederick, 1981, 1986) about using small groups and role playing. Here I will just sketch the outlines of this strategy. First, a minilecture, probably combined with a reading assignment, clearly establishes the context and setting. Second, the class is divided into small groups, each assigned clearly delineated roles in some historical or contemporary controversy: management-labor, urban interests, a political convention, and so forth. Third, each group is given a specific, concrete task—usually, to propose a position and a course of action ("Decide on three to five goals and three to five ways of achieving them"). The proposals emerging from different groups will inevitably conflict in some way—ideologically, tactically, racially, regionally, or with respect to scarce funds, land, jobs, power, or resources.

The format for role playing requires careful planning, clear instructions, assertive leadership, and a lot of luck. One might hear the proposals of different groups and immediately incorporate them into a lecture, or one could organize a meeting or convention to consider the proposals. The groups might, for example, be instructed to prepare speeches and see the deliberations through to some conclusion, caucusing to develop strategies, coalitions, and tactics for achieving their goals. As in real life, neat and simple closures are not easy, but this strategy has enormous potential for active learning.

The most important rule for role playing is that at least as much time should be taken in debriefing as was used in the activity itself, for this is when the substantive learning occurs. With either groups or dyads, role playing has the affective power of theater. A lot of emotion is generated: anger, frustration, joy, tension, warmth. Emotions, if not excessive, focus attention, trigger memories, and heighten performance. The debriefing session, therefore, is crucial to helping students translate affective experience into cognitive learning.

Media. The same emotional process happens with the use of media in the classroom: a film or videotape, a short dramatic scene or the reading of some well-chosen quotations, a set of slides, music, or some combination. A synchronized slide-tape presentation, for example, with each lyrical line of a musical piece being paired with a visual image, has tremendous power to evoke emotions and can be used to motivate, to hook the student world with ours, to introduce or summarize critical course themes, and to concretize ideas, raise questions, and deepen analysis. In each case, learning results from the juxtaposition of emotions and cognitive thought.

In advising departmental colleagues to try out these strategies for involving students, caution them not to change all at once or be too fancy. By trying out only a few new strategies, we discover those we feel comfortable with and over time develop a bigger bag of tricks. Also, chairpersons need to make room for some failure. The first time we try something, it often does not work. The chances of success are raised if we tell our students that we are experimenting with a new teaching strategy. Being open about our enthusiasm and uncertainties, we establish a bond with students' own feelings and desire to succeed, which enlists their support in making it work. Finally, if chairpersons try out new strategies themselves, they will deepen bonds with their colleagues and help to improve the quality of student learning.

References

Chickering, A., and Gamson, Z. "Seven Principles for Good Practice in Undergraduate Education." *AAHE Bulletin,* 1987, *39* (7), 3-7.

Cross, K. P. "The Adventures of Education in Wonderland: Implementing Education Reform." *Phi Delta Kappan,* 1987, *68* (7), 498-499.

Fong, B. "Commonplaces About Teaching: Second Thoughts." *Change,* 1987, *19* (4), 28-29.

Frederick, P. "The Dreaded Discussion: Ten Ways to Start." *Improving College and University Teaching,* 1981, *29* 109-114.

Frederick, P. "The Lively Lecture—Eight Variations." *College Teaching,* 1986, *34* (2), 43-50.

Peter J. Frederick is professor of history and chairperson of the Division of Social Science at Wabash College, Crawfordsville, Indiana.

Knowing how students reason and how to foster discipline-specific skills in critical thinking helps chairpersons respond positively to faculty concerns about students' reasoning deficiencies.

Helping Faculty Foster Students' Critical Thinking in the Disciplines

Joanne Gainen Kurfiss

"We worked in small groups a lot, even though the class was held in an auditorium. But we managed OK." "Johnson had us writing all the time! But it really helped me learn. And my writing has improved, too." "The class always seemed to be in an uproar. Seems like everything we studied in there was controversial, and everyone had to have a say. We listened to each other, though. And the professor always seemed interested in what we had to say."

Comments like these from students signal to you as chairperson the presence in your department of professors who are helping students learn to think critically. They may be professors of psychology or music or accounting or zoology, but they are also professors of thinking.

These faculty members probably perform quite respectably on departmental teacher-rating forms, although they are not necessarily star performers. The methods they use are unconventional and therefore disconcerting to some students. For example, they may not lecture much, preferring to use class time to stimulate students' thinking through discussion, problem solving, or experiential exercises. Student rating forms that emphasize instructor presentation skills (clarity, organization,

A. F. Lucas (ed.). *The Department Chairperson's Role in Enhancing College Teaching.*
New Directions for Teaching and Learning, no. 37. San Francisco: Jossey-Bass, Spring 1989.

enthusiasm) betray a bias toward classrooms in which the professor is the authority and students receive knowledge passively from lectures supplemented by texts. Many students share that bias, but it is difficult, perhaps impossible, for students to develop critical thinking when the professor is doing all the thinking.

How do these professors challenge their students so successfully? What can the chairperson do to facilitate their work? What can be done to encourage other faculty to develop their own approaches to teaching critical thinking? After exploring the nature of critical thinking and its development, we will take up each of these questions in turn.

Critical Thinking in the Disciplines

Critical thinking is the process of figuring out what to believe or do about a situation, phenomenon, problem, or controversy for which no single definitive answer or solution exists. The term implies a diligent, open-minded search for understanding, rather than for discovery of a necessary conclusion. The issue explored may be academic, practical, esthetic, or ethical. Critical thinking is usually associated with education, but it is essential to rational living in the workplace, in politics, and in personal relationships (Brookfield, 1987).

The particular content, form, and standards of reasoning involved in critical thinking vary by discipline. For example, social scientists search for causes of problems, to understand them and provide a basis for solutions. Literary critics examine textual or biographical evidence and the cultural context of a work, to help them develop an interpretation.

In spite of clear differences among the disciplines, common elements of reasoning exist. Critical thinking in all disciplines involves both discovery and justification of ideas. In the discovery phase, we examine evidence in search of patterns and formulate interpretations or hypotheses about what the evidence means. In the justification phase, we set forth our conclusions, reasoning, and evidence in an argument.

The Challenge of Teaching Thinking

Professors frequently assign tasks that require critical thinking—for example, term papers, critiques, experiments, and case studies. Some students do quite well on such assignments. Others, however, produce disappointing results. Why is this so?

By virtue of their intimate familiarity with the questions and methods of their disciplines, professors are uniquely qualified to help students develop thinking skills required for success in their courses. However, this familiarity may also block professors' understanding of their students' struggle to reason in the context of a discipline that is unfamiliar to them. Experts' reasoning in their disciplines is so automatic that they are often unaware of it. Teaching students to think means making this tacit knowledge explicit and experimenting with teaching methods, to help students develop some skill in tackling representative problems in a discipline.

Department chairpersons can play a key role by persuading faculty that teaching for thinking is important and by supporting and rewarding professors of thinking. The department will benefit from the renewed vitality such teaching can engender.

Critical-Thinking Abilities

Students' critical-thinking abilities are not well developed when they enter college. Moreover, the influence of college experiences on reasoning is disappointingly small. For example, the idea that an opinion or claim must be supported by a well-reasoned argument is a minority view prior to graduate school. Seniors are only slightly less prone than freshmen to believe that opinions are based on individual preferences, as opposed to evidence (King, Kitchener, and Wood, 1985). Similarly, the depth of argument students offer in support of their positions on an issue is minimal; it increases only slightly between the freshman and senior years (Perkins, 1985).

Several characteristics of students' thinking make it difficult for them to achieve unaided the high standards of reasoning educators envision for them.

Knowledge Base for Thinking. Students lack the abundant and well-organized knowledge base that provides essential raw material for reasoning (Larkin, Heller, and Greeno, 1980). The knowledge they do have is often poorly organized and may contain misconceptions. Because students frequently acquire new knowledge by rote-memory strategies, much of what they "know" is inert and therefore not accessible for use in argumentation or problem solving. As newcomers to the field, students are only beginning to accumulate and organize knowledge needed to reason about the topic.

In addition to acquiring information about the topic, called *declarative knowledge,* students must learn procedures for answering questions in the discipline. *Procedural knowledge* is knowledge of how to do things in the discipline. In mathematics or engineering, this means knowing how to solve problems. In other disciplines, procedural knowledge includes knowing how to resolve conflicts in management; how to identify rocks in geology or plants in botany; how to interpret, criticize, or produce a painting or sculpture in art, or a poem, play, short story, or novel in literature.

Much procedural knowledge is tacit, difficult to articulate and even more difficult for students to discover on their own. In the context of discovery, tacit procedural knowledge consists of the discipline's methods of inquiry. What kinds of questions characterize the discipline? How do people in the field find answers to their questions? How do they go about evaluating previous research? Although these are valued skills, we rarely teach them deliberately. Students must figure them out for themselves—a slow and unnecessarily frustrating process.

Procedural knowledge in the realm of justification is knowledge of how to present an argument in the field. Is evidence presented in descriptive or narrative form? Is problem solution the preferred form? Thesis-supporting reasons? Hypothesis-experiment-findings-discussion? Theorem-proof? These are variations on the basic argument form. Students are not generally aware of these macrostructures of argument. By pointing them out in various readings and highlighting them in instructions for assignments, the professor gives students a valuable tool to support their learning in the field.

Beliefs About Knowledge

Many students hold beliefs about knowledge that conflict with the goals of critical thinking. These beliefs have been described by Perry (1970, 1981) and by Belenky, Clinchy, Goldberger, and Tarule (1986). These influential formulations reveal a progression in students' understanding of indeterminacy and pluralism. At each level of the progression, students respond differently to assignments and class activities that depend on critical thinking.

Level 1: Dualism/Received Knowledge. At this level, students equate knowledge with factual information; to learn is to acquire information from the professor and the text. Facts are seen as either correct or not; hence, Perry's (1970, 1981) label for this belief system is *dualism.* The professor is an authority who presents truth. Level 1 students' dependence on authority led Belenky, Clinchy, Goldberger, and Tarule (1986) to refer to this perspective as *received knowledge.*

These students may become confused or indignant when professors ask them to interpret or criticize ideas. Facts are facts, in this view; there is no room for interpretation. Such students are probably most comfortable learning from informative, entertaining lectures free of ambiguities and conflicting theories.

Level 2: Multiplicity/Subjective Knowledge. Most students soon come to recognize the existence of doubts and uncertainties in some areas of knowledge. Where the facts are not known, knowledge is a matter of mere opinion, and one opinion is as good as another. Perry's (1970, 1981) term *multiplicity* suggests an early, uncritical view of pluralism. Belenky, Clinchy, Goldberger, and Tarule's (1986) term *subjective knowing* accents the appeal to inner standards of truth that characterizes this perspective.

Students at this level often object to grading on matters of opinion. They may complain that a weak paper received a low grade because the professor disagreed with them; they fail to recognize that the opinion it expresses is not well supported. Level 2 is the dominant epistemology among today's undergraduates (Belenky, Clinchy, Goldberger, and Tarule, 1986; King, Kitchener, and Wood, 1985).

Level 3: Relativism/Procedural Knowledge. Insistent pressure to provide reasons for their opinions helps students to realize that supported opinions are better than mere opinions. They learn to analyze issues, problems, texts, or works of art and to marshal evidence in support of their conclusions about them. The term *procedural knowledge* reflects the students' recognition that disciplines teach special procedures for reasoning. In time, students may realize that this academic method of deciding issues applies to most or all disciplines. Perry (1970, 1981) labels this belief system *relativism*, because it takes as axiomatic that knowledge is relative to the frame of reference of the knower.

Level 4: Commitment in Relativism/Constructed Knowledge. Relativistic procedural analysis may illuminate a situation, but it does not provide definitive answers. Ultimately, we must take a position and make commitments, even though we can have no external assurances of the correctness of what we choose to do or believe—hence, Perry's (1970, 1981) term *commitment in relativism*. Constructed knowing integrates knowledge learned from others with the inner truth of experience and personal reflection (Belenky, Clinchy, Goldberger, and Tarule, 1986).

Of these belief systems, only levels 3 and 4 support critical thinking. Critical thinking requires students to recognize the indeterminacy of knowledge and learn procedures for making sense of multiple possibilities for belief and action.

These characteristics of students provide the context in which professors of thinking operate. Many educators intuitively recognize the constraints imposed by students' limited declarative and procedural knowledge and by the belief systems referred to here as levels 1 and 2. Some have devised ways to help students overcome these constraints.

Overcoming Students' Limitations

Paradoxically, many of the limitations on students' thinking abilities can be overcome by designing assignments that require them to think. Professors of thinking provide intellectual resources, in addition to information to support students' efforts to meet the challenges of such assignments. Support may be designed to strengthen students' knowledge base, to develop procedural knowledge, or to modify students' beliefs about knowledge.

Knowledge Base. To improve students' knowledge base for thinking, instruction should aim for students' understanding, rather than for instructors' coverage of declarative knowledge. This means setting broad goals for understanding key concepts and maintaining a flexible agenda to allow for dialogue and corrective feedback (Collins and Stevens, 1982). Students must share the burdens of preparation for this approach to work. To ensure preparation, a professor of organizational behavior gives quizzes on reading materials at the beginning of each unit. Students take the quiz individually first, turn in their results, and then take it as part of a permanent team. Team discussions clarify most concepts, freeing remaining class time for more difficult concepts and extensions of the material (Michaelsen, 1983).

Short writing assignments help students organize and clarify their knowledge, so that they can use it in subsequent reasoning situations. Writing brief analytical essays based on readings increases students' learning, particularly when their initial level of knowledge is low. Writing essays also gives students practice in analytical reasoning in the discipline. These assignments need not be graded, although the professor may want to look them over and provide group feedback (for examples in many disciplines, see Griffin, 1982).

Procedural Knowledge. This must be rehearsed, with feedback, to become part of the students' knowledge base. Investigative tasks foster a rudimentary grasp of inquiry methods while acquainting students with important problems and information in the field. Tasks can be sequenced from brief, concrete, highly structured exercises toward more complex, abstract, and independent investigations. Standards for evaluating students' work may also be raised, as their knowledge of the subject and their familiarity with its forms of inquiry increase.

In mathematics and physics, researchers have found that experts identify principles underlying a problem before they apply an equation (Schoenfeld, 1985; Larkin, Heller, and Greeno, 1980). Instruction in problem analysis can be incorporated into problem sessions or lectures. Demonstrating the processes of reasoning (studying the problem, planning an approach, reviewing progress, and verifying results) counteracts students' tendency to apply equations before they understand the problem.

In engineering, too, students must learn to analyze problems, identify constraints, generate and evaluate alternatives, and decide on solutions. A professor of chemical engineering teaches a decision-making model to students in the introductory course. Students work in teams to learn methods they will employ throughout their professional careers.

The model, called *guided design,* has been adapted for use in dozens of other disciplines (Wales, Nardi, and Stager, 1986).

Arguments are a common feature of reasoning in all domains, although they take different forms. A psychology professor teaches students a model for analyzing arguments in psychology. Students use the model to sort out evidence and conclusions in articles they read, and the professor uses the model to provide feedback on students' papers (Cerbin, 1988).

Conducting field research requires knowledge of how to observe, record, and interpret behavioral information. In an undergraduate course on children's communication skills, students learn fieldwork methods and use them to observe children and adolescents in such real-world settings as schools, parks, and clubs. In class, they discuss their findings and integrate them with material from texts and lectures (Wulff and Nyquist, 1988). These methods provide essential practice in reasoning and foster understanding, involvement, and motivation to learn.

Beliefs About Knowledge. Beliefs about knowledge can be influenced toward greater complexity by challenging students' simplistic conceptions while supporting their attempts to understand complexity. An optimal match is a course that presents intellectual challenges at a level just beyond students' current beliefs and offers support at the students' present level.

Since most students hold level 1 or level 2 beliefs, instruction designed for these levels will probably address the needs of the majority. At level 1, challenge arises when students are asked to look at issues in diverse and sometimes conflicting ways. Support is found in clear, authoritative explanations, outlines, instructions, and help in clarifying theoretical material. Summarizing opposing positions on an issue is a challenge for level 1 students, but it can be supported by class discussion and feedback. At level 2, requests to support or evaluate opinions are challenging. Support is provided by freedom to express opinions and explicit criteria for evaluation. A caring professor and a positive classroom environment provide needed support at any level.

To meet the needs of students at levels 1 and 2 simultaneously, a political science professor introduces three perspectives on an issue. For example, students study the Cuban missile crisis from the point of view of the United States, the Soviet Union, and Cuba. Students first attempt to understand each view on its own terms. After hearing all three views, they present their own conclusions and reasoning. The challenge of learning and evaluating three perspectives is supported by a clear framework for inquiry and by students' knowledge that they need not relinquish their initial views. The activity changes few minds but increases students' appreciation of diversity (Freie, 1987).

Common Themes for Teaching Thinking

These examples illustrate the accelerating effort in higher education to find new ways to educate students for critical thinking (see Kurfiss, 1988, for a review). Across disciplines, approaches to teaching thinking share several features worth noting.

1. *Explicit identification of desired thinking skills.* The course is organized around what students must do with their knowledge.

2. *Practice and feedback on students' attempts to use thinking skills before the final graded performance.* Frequently used methods include ungraded writing, small-group work, and examples.

3. *Respect for students and responsiveness to their developmental capabilities.*

4. *Graded critical-thinking activities.* Criteria for evaluating students' work are public and explicit, and examples are discussed when the assignment is given.

5. *Active students and a facilitative professor.*

Supporting Professors of Thinking

Recognize and congratulate professors of thinking in your department. Talk with them about their teaching. When you visit their classes, notice specific strategies they use, and ask about them later. Invite them to discuss their teaching with other interested faculty. They may find that discussion of their colleagues' questions helps them understand questions of their own.

Encourage these professors to document the effects of their teaching on the quality of students' reasoning, knowledge acquisition, and attitudes toward the discipline. Give them merit raises and promotion recommendations based on evidence of effectiveness in developing students' thinking skills and the inclination to think critically.

Many teachers who address thinking processes assign a great deal of writing, and so providing assistants to read early drafts of students' papers or to do library work reduces the burdens of grading. Some institutions have programs in which advanced undergraduates or honors students fill this role, either for credit or for payment.

Offer to buy a departmental subscription to a journal on teaching, and ask them to make suggestions. Invite them to recommend books on teaching for the departmental library. Ask if they would be willing to present their ideas to other faculty on campus. If so, recommend them to campus organizers of teaching seminars and workshops. Encourage them to write about what they are doing in their classes. Offer to support their attendance at conferences on critical thinking.

Developing Faculty Interest in Teaching Critical Thinking

In your role as department chairperson, you probably hear faculty express many concerns about students' reasoning abilities, often in the form of complaints. The analysis offered here will help you reinterpret complaints about students' deficiencies in developmental terms. An understanding of students' problems can prompt renewed interest in teaching on the part of faculty members whose optimism and energy are flagging in that area.

To stimulate conversation about teaching for thinking, encourage faculty to share their strategies for helping students learn to think about the disciplines. Circulate copies of short articles on teaching for critical thinking and other higher-order outcomes. Encourage faculty to write their responses, and pass them along with the article. Collect favorites and circulate them, perhaps with a brief prefacing statement explaining who suggested the article and why, or circulate a list of favorites and keep it on hand in the department for borrowing or copying.

Create opportunities for faculty to talk informally and positively about their teaching. Many faculty find constructive discussions of teaching unexpectedly stimulating. There is always much to puzzle over in teaching, be it a specific student, unanticipated responses to an assignment or exercise, or plans for a new class. Faculty may find that they enjoy talking about whatever is puzzling them at the moment. Their discussions can lead to further conversations and inquiry and, ultimately, to changes toward more inquiry-centered classrooms.

If your campus has a teaching-improvement program, let the staff know of your interest in critical thinking. Some centers can also provide workshops tailored specifically to a department. Put together a team of faculty to attend a conference on critical thinking (resources permitting). Teaching-improvement centers can sometimes offer funds to support attendance at such conferences.

Organize a faculty project team to examine your curriculum from the point of view of developing critical thinking in students. What kinds of reasoning skills do particular courses invoke? What kinds of difficulties do students seem to have at various points in the curriculum? Which aspects of the content lend themselves to inquiry methods? Even though a major curriculum revision may not result, this kind of discussion may prompt individual faculty to find new ways to encourage and facilitate critical thinking in their courses.

50

References

Belenky, M. F., Clinchy, B. M., Goldberger, N. R., and Tarule, J. M. *Women's Ways of Knowing: The Development of Self, Voice, and Mind.* New York: Basic Books, 1986.

Brookfield, S. D. *Developing Critical Thinkers: Challenging Adults to Explore Alternative Ways of Thinking and Acting.* San Francisco: Jossey-Bass, 1987.

Cerbin, B. "The Nature and Development of Informal Reasoning Skills in College Students." Paper presented at the twelfth national University of Chicago Institute on Issues in Teaching and Learning, Chicago, April 24-27, 1988.

Collins, A., and Stevens, A. L. "Goals and Strategies of Inquiry Teachers." In R. Glaser (ed.), *Advances in Instructional Psychology.* Vol. 2. Hillsdale, N.J.: Erlbaum, 1982.

Freie, J. F. "Thinking and Believing." *College Teaching,* 1987, *35* (3), 89-91.

Griffin, C. W. (ed.). *Teaching Writing in All Disciplines.* New Directions for Teaching and Learning, no. 12. San Francisco: Jossey-Bass, 1982.

King, P. M., Kitchener, K. S., and Wood, P. K. "The Development of Intellect and Character: A Longitudinal-Sequential Study of Intellectual and Moral Development in Young Adults." *Moral Education Forum,* 1985, *10* (1), 1-13.

Kurfiss, J. G. *Critical Thinking: Theory, Research, Practice, and Possibilities.* Washington, D.C.: Association for the Study of Higher Education, 1988.

Larkin, J. H., Heller, J. I., and Greeno, J. G. "Instructional Implications of Research on Problem Solving." In W. J. McKeachie (ed.), *Learning, Cognition, and College Teaching.* New Directions for Teaching and Learning, no. 2. San Francisco: Jossey-Bass, 1980.

Michaelsen, L. "Team Learning in Large Classes." In C. Bouton and R. Y. Garth (eds.), *Learning in Groups.* New Directions for Teaching and Learning, no. 14. San Francisco: Jossey-Bass, 1983.

Perkins, D. N. "Postprimary Education Has Little Impact on Informal Reasoning." *Journal of Educational Psychology,* 1985, *77* (5), 562-571.

Perry, W. G., Jr. *Forms of Intellectual and Ethical Development in the College Years: A Scheme.* New York: Holt, Rinehart & Winston, 1970.

Perry, W. G., Jr. "Cognitive and Ethical Growth: The Making of Meaning." In A. W. Chickering and Associates, *The Modern American College: Responding to the New Realities of Diverse Students and a Changing Society.* San Francisco: Jossey-Bass, 1981.

Schoenfeld, A. H. *Mathematical Problem Solving.* New York: Academic Press, 1985.

Wales, C. E., Nardi, A. H., and Stager, R. A. *Professional Decision Making.* Morgantown, W.Va.: University Center for Guided Design, 1986.

Wulff, D., and Nyquist, J. "Using Field Methods as an Instructional Tool." In J. G. Kurfiss, L. Hilsen, S. Kahn, M. D. Sorcinelli, and R. Tiberius (eds.), *To Improve the Academy.* Vol. 7. Stillwater, Okla.: POD/New Forums Press, 1988.

Joanne Gainen Kurfiss is a teaching consultant in the Center for Teaching Effectiveness at the University of Delaware.

Amidst national calls for more effective higher education,
problem-based learning is gaining in popularity. What is it?
What skills and attitudes are required of teachers?

Problem-Based Learning: One Approach to Increasing Student Participation

LuAnn Wilkerson, Grahame Feletti

The day-to-day demands of managing an academic department can leave little time for examining and supporting the actions of individual faculty members as teachers. For the most part, faculty members plan and teach their courses in the privacy of their own classrooms—unless a student complaint reaches the chairperson's office. Although no one would argue that the chairperson should attempt to tell the faculty members how or what to teach, there is a need for active leadership in shaping and guiding the teaching program of the department. Leadership in this area calls for knowledge about effective instructional practices, skills in motivating faculty members to examine and reexamine their teaching programs and methods, and the willingness to support teachers when they risk trying something new. It is to the first of these issues that the present chapter speaks—knowing more about effective instructional practices.

The National Institute of Education (1984) issued a report to address the question of how to maximize the learning and personal development of undergraduate students in colleges and universities. The educational leaders who compiled the report recommended three major changes in the structure and conduct of higher education.

A. F. Lucas (ed.). *The Department Chairperson's Role in Enhancing College Teaching.*
New Directions for Teaching and Learning, no. 37. San Francisco: Jossey-Bass, Spring 1989.

1. Students should be more actively involved in learning tasks. When they are, they learn more than when they are passive recipients of instruction. To accomplish this recommendation, changes are needed in institutional policies, as well as in the ways in which faculty members teach.

2. Institutions and individual teachers should clearly communicate the requirements, standards, and objectives of learning. This suggests that from the institutional mission to the goals for the various majors to the objectives of individual courses, such decisions need to be purposefully and thoughtfully made and explicitly communicated to students. Learning is maximized when we make it clear to students what is to be accomplished and why.

3. Assessment and feedback should be regular and systematic components of the learning process. Students learn what they practice, and if assessment comes only at the end of a course of study, errors can go uncorrected.

In this chapter, we will explore one specific approach to implementing these recommendations—problem-based learning. This approach has its roots in the discovery method of teaching promoted by John Dewey in the 1930s. It reappeared in the 1960s as the inquiry approach to teaching science, heavily influenced by the work of Jerome Bruner and Jean Piaget. Currently, problem-based learning has been the subject of a great deal of attention in medical education, as Harvard Medical School has engaged in revising its preclinical curriculum from a lecture-based to a problem-based format.

Problem-Based Learning

The problem-based movement in medical education was begun at McMaster University in the mid 1970s. According to Barrows and Tamblyn (1980):

> Problem-based learning is the learning that results from the process of working toward the understanding or resolution of a problem. The problem is encountered *first* in the learning process. There is nothing new about the use of problem solving as a method of learning in a variety of educational settings. Unlike what occurs in real-life situations, however, the problem usually is not given to the student first, as a stimulus for active learning. It usually is given to the student after he has been provided with facts or principles, either as an example of the importance of this knowledge or as an exercise in which the student can apply this knowledge [pp. 1–2].

Problems can be incorporated into a variety of classroom formats: small-group collaborative activities, large-group case method discussion, laboratory experimentation, interactive lecturing, or computer-assisted independent study. The crucial components are that the problems raise compelling issues for new learning and that students have an opportunity to become actively involved in the discussion of these issues, with appropriate feedback and corrective assistance from faculty members. The problems are not viewed as mere supplements to lecture but stand as a centerpiece of the educational experience. In working with the problems, students are expected to draw on previous learning and experience, to pose questions concerning new issues, to set personal learning goals, to take responsibility for their own learning through independent reading and study, and to teach one another through student-to-student discussion.

Involvement in Learning

Problem-based learning increases student participation in learning tasks. Regardless of the particular classroom format, the problem-based approach encourages students to work through some variation of the following process (Schmidt, 1983) as they learn essential concepts, factual information, and ways of thinking in the discipline:

1. *Confronting the problem* by identifying its nature and extent; identifying possible procedures to use in resolving it; generating possible hypotheses, either general or specific, to explain or resolve it; requesting additional data that may support or challenge the proposed hypotheses; identifying questions for additional self-study; and determining how to proceed with that study.

2. *Engaging in independent study* by selecting and locating resources; managing information overload, with the help of critical reading and information technology; structuring time to allow for effective and efficient use of resources; developing active study strategies, including peer discussion, note taking, charting, computer management of information, self-quizzing, and so forth; and participating in scheduled lectures and other related learning opportunities, with particular questions in mind.

3. *Returning to the problem* by sharing new learning and tackling continuing questions with other students; examining and prioritizing original hypotheses in light of new learning; selecting and critiquing potential solutions; raising new questions for additional study; and summarizing, organizing, and synthesizing what is now known.

The Teaching-Learning Encounter

The approach to be taken by the faculty member in problem-based learning also represents a radical departure from the more traditional definition of teaching. In problem-based learning, objectives are collaboratively set by students, with the assistance of the teacher. Students actively participate in teaching one another both new information and ways of thinking, with the teacher providing some combination of challenge and support (Daloz, 1986).

Control—typically exerted by the teacher over class time, objectives, and content—manifests itself differently in problem-based learning. The primary mechanism for the teacher to exercise control of the learning situation is the selection and crafting of the problems. What questions should students be asking in the course? What problems will provoke them to raise those questions?

Critical-thinking skills develop best under conditions that encourage students to synthesize and verbalize ideas, without punishment or fear of making mistakes. Many problem-based learning curricula rely on a small-group format, in which students have multiple opportunities to ask questions and to provide in-depth explanations to one another (Webb, 1982). However, it is worth reiterating that critical-thinking skills can be developed through large-group discussions and carefully crafted independent study assignments. It will not be done effectively with any method, unless students can interact constructively, without feeling a need to perform or to remain quiet as a self-defense.

Selecting Problems. The most compelling problems are real ones that stimulate students to search for possible explanations and solutions. Details of a real problem can be highlighted, deleted, or elaborated on, depending on the questions the instructor wishes to provoke. Beginning students might benefit from simple, well-structured representations, in which the understanding of a set of rules and principles leads to a straightforward solution. Learners with more experience in the area under study might be ready to tackle complex, ill-structured, "messy" problems. In either case, the selection and crafting of the problems represents the major way in which the teacher controls the learning that is to take place. Once a problem is encountered by the students, they take responsibility for their own learning.

Collins and Stevens (1983) studied transcripts from fourteen inquiry teachers at all levels of education and found that they purposefully selected problems to include both positive and negative exemplars and to demonstrate the effect of holding one variable constant while varying others. These teachers followed a pattern in their choice of cases, illustrating the most important, concrete, and frequently occurring concepts first.

Educational Benefits. A number of educational benefits are attributed to the various features of problem-based learning (Andre, 1986; Barrows and Tamblyn, 1980; Boud, 1986; Wales, 1977). First, by taking responsibility for their own learning, students develop learning strategies and habits that will serve them well for a lifetime of learning, particularly when they encounter unfamiliar problems. Glaser (1984) labels these *self-regulatory* or *metacognitive* skills: knowing what one knows and does not know, predicting outcomes, planning ahead, efficiently apportioning time and cognitive resources, and monitoring one's efforts to solve a problem or learn.

In problem-based learning, students can no longer rely on the teacher to cover all the important material in the course. Instead, students are encouraged to generate their own learning issues and to set priorities for learning with the help of the teacher. This experience can give them confidence in pursuing self-directed learning and in assessing their own performance long after they graduate.

This educational approach typically captures and enhances students' motivation to learn. Problems provide relevance and raise dissonance that demands resolution. Active participation in defining, resolving, or managing a problem points up the need to acquire new information, attitudes, and skills. Certainly, there is evidence that students do find this approach to learning quite satisfying (Clarke, Engel, and Feletti, 1984; Kaufman, 1985). When a problem-based approach is implemented across an entire institution, students develop learning styles commensurate with that approach and different from those styles demonstrated by students in a more traditional curriculum (Newble and Clarke, 1986).

In attempting to solve problems, students develop the ability to think with and about disciplinary concepts. They may also develop more generic reasoning processes, which transfer to similar situations. For example, in the sciences, these processes might include the ability to form initial hypotheses, collect data to test those hypotheses, and evaluate possible solutions. Previous learning is restructured by the learner as he or she attempts to accommodate new information, and new learning is organized for assimilation into existing knowledge structures. In solving problems, learners acquire two types of knowledge—knowledge of concepts, principles and facts; and procedures for how to use them. Too often, instruction focuses only on the first type of knowledge, while assuming that procedures for using that knowledge develop automatically.

Different Formats for Problem-Based Learning

Although the original description of problem-based learning in medical education focused on the use of small groups with a faculty tutor, the approach can be applied in a number of different educational settings.

Small-Group Discussion with a Faculty Tutor. Students meet with a faculty member who serves as a facilitator and occasional expert resource in their discussion of problems. This format is the one used in the New Pathway curriculum at Harvard Medical School and the arts and sciences tutorials at Harvard College.

Collaborative Learning Groups. Students meet together, without a teacher as a member of the group. Meetings usually occur in the classroom, where the teacher can serve as a consultant, as needed. Collaborative groups might also work outside class.

Case Method Teaching. This method, frequently used in business and law schools, engages a large group of students (seventy-five to one hundred) in the discussion of a problem that has been carefully analyzed by students prior to the class session, often through study in informal peer groups. Class discussion is carefully orchestrated by a faculty member, to promote critical analysis, exploration of multiple perspectives, application of newly learned ideas, and the making of well-supported decisions (Christensen and Hansen, 1987).

Case-Based Lectures. The teacher begins a lecture with a case for discussion by the class. The case is used to raise interest in the topic of the lecture and to encourage students to activate their existing knowledge base as a first step in learning new material. The teacher uses student comments in the lecture that follows the discussion (Barrows, Myers, Williams, and Moticka, 1986).

Inquiry Labs. Rather than follow a "cookbook" assignment in lab, students encounter problems that require the deduction of new concepts or that engage them in the design and implementation of simple experiments. The teacher is available as a consultant.

Independent Study. Students can work alone on problems, using computer-assisted instruction, audiovisual resources, books, and journals. Students take an active role in determining the content, materials, and timing of the instruction. Occasional meetings with a faculty tutor provide for discussion, assessment, and feedback.

Almost any kind of classroom format can be adapted to a problem-based approach to learning, if problems are introduced to students before all the requisite information has been provided by the teacher, if active participation is encouraged, and if students are allowed some control over the goals, processes, and pace of learning.

Setting Clear and High Expectations

Problem-based learning methods can also be useful in setting clear and challenging expectations for students. At least two generations of teachers in higher education have been inculcated in the ritual of using instructional objectives for this purpose (Mager, 1984). Specific behavioral wording has been considered essential, not only to indicate clearly what the students will gain from the course but also to provide a framework for examinations.

While this strategy is intellectually honest and tells the student in a straightforward way what is to be learned during a particular course, comprehensive lists of carefully worded learning objectives reinforce teacher direction and control. By contrast, those teachers who fail to offer anything but the most vaguely worded statements about academic growth and understanding are likely to frustrate students and administrators.

Obviously, some form of compromise must be reached, since teachers are ultimately accountable for their students' progress. Problem-based educators advocate two useful approaches to setting clear and high expectations, without undue adherence to any extreme. One step is to work at the institutional or departmental level to establish generic or overall program competencies, which can be tested at the end of an entire educational program. Program competencies can be written to emphasize broad subject areas, themes, or educational domains, such as those developed by the Newcastle Medical School in Australia (Engle and Clarke, 1979) and Alverno College in Milwaukee, Wisconsin. At Newcastle, five skill domains (covering forty-six generic competencies) serve as the basis of instruction throughout the school: self-directed learning; population medicine; professional skills; critical reasoning; and identification, prevention, and management of illness. These competencies also form the basis of end-of-program examinations, with students expected to pass in each of the domains in order to graduate (Feletti, Saunders, and Smith, 1983). Specific courses or groups of courses might emulate this domain-based structure while also teaching and testing course-specific knowledge and skills. When used across an entire degree program, with the cooperation of various course teachers, this approach can provide longitudinal profiles on students' academic growth and indicate subject-specific development.

Another approach involves setting high and clear expectations for student performance within each course, using a variant form of objectives. Rather than stating, and then trying to teach and assess, rigid and detailed lists of knowledge, skills, and attitudes, the teacher prepares a list of guiding questions, which students should be able to answer after their study of a particular problem, unit of instruction, or course. Students should be encouraged to generate lists of guiding questions for themselves during the study and discussion of a problem. Such a list can be compared to that of the teacher after a period of student-directed work, to ensure that students have tackled the major issues in the problem. This approach allows the teacher to provide a sense of direction, without giving answers and discouraging inquiry on the part of the students.

Adequate Assessment and Feedback

Problem-based learning has inherent advantages for teachers who want to give more regular and effective feedback than that based on more traditional examination schedules. First, students' greater participation in class gives teachers and the students themselves more data to use in judging performance. In discussions with peers, students acquire further feedback, as they compare their understanding with that of others in the class. The teacher can also provide generalized feedback to students as a group about shared misperceptions or successes and hold individual conferences with students who appear to be having serious difficulties during discussions.

Second, teachers can also use problem-based learning to encourage students to assess their own learning. Discussion among peers allows learners to compare their answers to those of other students, to discover errors in thinking, and to hear correct solutions derived. In classroom activities and homework assignments, the teacher can ask questions that challenge students to assess themselves. During lectures, he or she can pose problems and encourage students to think aloud toward solutions, rather than to produce final "right" answers. The lecture can then be used to address conceptual difficulties or to raise alternative explanations (Brown, 1978). Some recent data suggest that such efforts in lectures can be as effective as small-group tutorials in developing problem-solving skills (Barrows, Myers, Williams, and Moticka, 1986). In small-group discussions, students can be encouraged to develop their own questions. Students can compare their own sets of questions to those of the teacher, thereby getting feedback on their capability to develop progressively more sophisticated questions about the subject matter of the course. Student self-assessment serves as an additional source of feedback to that provided by the teacher through regular examinations and graded assignments.

Teachers can also make effective use of problem-based learning at examination time by writing questions that test not only knowledge acquisition but also students' ability to use knowledge in solving important problems in the discipline. Students can be asked to justify decisions or explain relevant underlying principles. Examinations need not be restricted to traditional, supervised in-class forms. Open-book, take-home assessments or brief oral interviews enable students to demonstrate a wide range of skills and knowledge.

Whatever examination methods are used, it is important to provide adequate feedback on performance, rather than just an indication of whether answers are right or wrong. Giving model answers to questions, allowing students to discuss those answers and to suggest alternatives before marking occurs, and providing each student the opportunity to review his or her performance with the teacher are all consistent with giving students a more active role in their own education.

The Role of the Department Chairperson

Department chairpersons can play several roles in promoting problem-based teaching methods among their faculty: as catalysts for change, resource linkers, and facilitators. As catalysts, they can encourage faculty members to question their current practices, through individual feedback and departmental discussion of the role of student participation in learning. Until teachers experience some dissonance between what they are now doing in the classroom and what they might be doing instead, they will not consider alternative methods of teaching and learning. Another method of catalyzing interest in problem-based learning is to try out the methods in one's own classroom and invite others to observe.

Once the chairperson has catalyzed interest, his or her role is to identify faculty members who are ready to change, and to provide the resources—personal, financial, and informational—that will support the teacher in the replanning and experimentation process. Finally, the chairperson serves as a facilitator for change, smoothing the way by providing appropriate teaching spaces, schedules, and materials for conducting problem-based activities. Ultimately, the chairperson is responsible for establishing a collaborative departmental climate that supports innovation and tolerates initial confusion during periods of change.

While individual teachers may choose to adopt problem-based learning strategies in their classrooms, it is much more powerful if whole departments or even institutions change to that approach. Participation in class discussion, in the setting of learning goals, and in assessing learning outcomes can become the norm, rather than an anomaly.

References

Andre, T. *Cognitive Classroom Learning: Understanding, Thinking and Problem Solving*. New York: Academic Press, 1986.

Barrows, H. S., Myers, A., Williams, R. G., and Moticka, E. J. "Large-Group Problem-Based Learning: A Possible Solution for the 2 Sigma Problem." *Medical Teacher,* 1986, *8,* 325–331.

Barrows, H. S., and Tamblyn, R. *Problem-Based Learning*. New York: Springer, 1980.

Boud, D. (ed.). *Problem-Based Learning in Education for the Professions*. Sydney: University of New South Wales, 1986.

Brown, G. *Lecturing and Explaining*. London: Methuen, 1978.

Christensen, R. C., and Hansen, A. J. *Teaching and the Case Method*. Boston: Harvard Business School, 1987.

Clarke, R. M., Engel, C. E., and Feletti, G. I. "Student Perceptions of the

Learning Environment in a New Medical School." *Medical Education,* 1984, *18,* 321–325.

Collins, A., and Stevens, A. L. "A Cognitive Theory of Interactive Learning." In C. M. Reigeluth (ed.), *Instructional Design Theories and Models: An Overview.* Hillsdale, N.J.: Erlbaum, 1983.

Daloz, L. A. *Effective Teaching and Mentoring: Realizing the Transformational Power of Adult Learning Experiences.* San Francisco: Jossey-Bass, 1986.

Engel, C. E., and Clarke, R. M. "Medical Education with a Difference." *Programmed Learning and Educational Technology,* 1979, *16,* 70–87.

Feletti, G. I., Saunders, N. A., and Smith, A. J. "Comprehensive Assessment of Final-Year Medical Student Performance Based on Undergraduate Program Objectives." *The Lancet,* July 2, 1983, pp. 34–37.

Glaser, R. "Education and Thinking: The Role of Knowledge." *American Psychologist,* 1984, *39,* 93–104.

Kaufman, A. (ed.). *Implementing Problem-Based Learning in Medical Education.* New York: Springer, 1985.

Mager, R. F. *Preparing Instructional Objectives.* (2nd ed.) Belmont, Calif.: Pitman Learning, 1984.

National Institute of Education. Study Group on the Conditions of Excellence in American Higher Education. *Involvement in Learning: Realizing the Potential of American Higher Education.* Washington, D.C.: U.S. Department of Education, 1984.

Newble, D., and Clarke, R. M. "The Approaches to Learning of Students in a Traditional and in an Innovative Problem-Based Medical School." *Medical Education,* 1986, *20,* 267–273.

Schmidt, H. G. "Problem-Based Learning: Rationale and Description." *Medical Education,* 1983, *17,* 11–16.

Wales, C. E. *Guided Design.* Morgantown, W. Va.: University Center for Guided Design, 1977.

Webb, N. M. "Student Interaction and Learning in Small Groups." *Review of Educational Research,* 1982, *52,* 421–445.

LuAnn Wilkerson is director of faculty development for the Office of Educational Development at Harvard Medical School.

Grahame Feletti is director of curriculum development for the Office of Educational Development at Harvard Medical School.

Chairpersons and their departments need a different pedagogy to serve the increasing number of adult part-time learners.

Improving Learning for Adult Part-Time Students

Richard N. Ottaway

This chapter is intended to provide department chairpersons with an approach to an increasing population in higher education—adult part-time students. The special needs of those students challenge college faculty and administrators. Chairpersons and departments need to devise new curricula and teaching strategies that integrate classroom learning with the knowledge that adult students have already acquired through personal and occupational experience.

Why Focus on Adult Part-Time Students?

Part-time and adult students are enrolled in higher education in greater numbers than ever, and there is every indication that this trend will continue. Between 1974 and 1984, part-time students increased at a rate three times greater than the rate for full-time students, and persons thirty-five years and older showed the greatest increase in numbers of any age group (Ottinger, 1987, p. 42). Of all adults over the age of twenty-five, 4.3 percent took at least one course for credit during the past twelve months. Of those approximately six million persons, 60 percent took a course in a degree program: 33 percent in graduate schools, 40 percent in undergraduate schools, and 25 percent in two-year colleges. One

A. F. Lucas (ed.). *The Department Chairperson's Role in Enhancing College Teaching.*
New Directions for Teaching and Learning, no. 37. San Francisco: Jossey-Bass, Spring 1989.

surprising fact is that 50 percent of the degree courses were taken before 4 P.M., with the hours of 8, 9, and 10 A.M. being the most popular. While the most frequently taken courses are business, there are enough adult part-time students in other courses for all chairpersons to take notice of the composition of student enrollment and help faculty design courses to serve these students.

An Appropriate Learning Objective for Adult Learners

An old adage says that those in the doctor's waiting room are not only sick but also concerned about being sick. The implication is that patients are motivated on several levels to come to doctors. The same can be said about adult learners. They are in class not only to get credentials but also to learn in a significantly different way than younger, full-time students do. Zemke and Zemke (1981) go so far as to say, "Adults seek out learning experiences in order to cope with specific life-change events" (p. 45). My experience is that adult students want a fuller and more comprehensive learning experience than our usual pedagogy gives them.

Many educators are now using terms like *lifelong learning, learning society,* and *andragogy* to describe a learning philosophy different from the old notion that a college operates from September to June with full-time students who are there for a once-in-a-lifetime experience. A fundamental step each department chairperson has to take in this new situation is to articulate appropriate objectives of education for the adult learner.

Argyris and Schön (1974) see the outcome of learning experiences as making theory more congruent with practice. This is an important objective for adult learners. Theory, which Argyris and Schön call "espoused theory," is what one intends to do. Practice, which they call "theory-in-use," is one's actual behavior. An appropriate objective for adult learners might be to get their theories—what they intend to do— more congruent with what they actually do. Adult part-time students have an excellent opportunity to work for congruity of theory and practice, because they are at the same time in the classroom for theory and in the workplace or life experience for practice.

Single-loop learning and double-loop learning are also useful concepts from the work of Argyris and Schön (1974). Single-loop learning is learning just what is expected. It is the typical learning in most educational settings: Learn the facts, give them back in order to get a grade, and receive the credential. Double-loop learning is investigating underlying assumptions and tying theory and practice together, which is analogous to critical thinking.

In later research, Argyris (1982) found that single-loop learning is typical of learning in most work organizations. He says, "We must not forget that the strategy of all organizations is to decompose double-loop problems into single-loop ones. The major part of everyday life in an organization is related to single-loop learning. Double-loop learning is crucial, however, because it allows us to examine and correct the way we are dealing with any issue and our underlying assumptions about it" (pp. 159–160). If we accept Argyris's conclusions, we can assume that the adult part-time learner will be coming from an environment that does not support investigative, critical thinking in practice, even if it espouses such thinking.

Argyris's thinking has profound implications for department chairpersons who want to increase the learning of adult part-time learners. The younger student expects (and has been led to expect) single-loop learning in the classroom. Adult learners come to school for something else. This may be true because of a life-event, which has prompted them to come to school (or, more often, return to school), dissatisfaction with the single-loop environment of the workplace, or increased awareness of the limitations of single-loop learning.

Argyris and Schön, along with others interested in adult learning, are developing concepts and educational processes that link the classroom and the workplace, the university and the world, the theory and the practice, so that the learner will be able to function more effectively—learn from practice, investigate and challenge every action— in all aspects of life. This seems to be an objective that chairpersons can use to develop teaching methods for the adult part-time learners in our departments. The rest of this chapter describes and discusses a pedagogy developed for adult part-time learners and based on the theories of Argyris and Schön.

A Proposed Pedagogy

Adapted from an earlier proposal for management students (Ottaway, 1985), this pedagogy can be used for teaching theories or skills to adult learners in many fields. There are four parts to this proposed learning cycle: learning a theory or skill in class, gathering data through observation or practicing the new skill in the workplace, reporting back and teaching fellow students, and writing an analytical critique.

Students enroll in a course with single-loop learning expectations. A new learning expectation must be created. The appropriate teaching style can set the stage for double-loop, reflective learning to take place. There are a number of characteristics of the learning situation under an instructor's control. The most important are *subject matter, group size, task definition,* and *degree of teacher monitoring* (Ottaway, in press). For single-loop, noncritical classroom learning, the teacher will use specific and narrowly defined subject matter, teach large groups of students at one time, have a very specific task definition of the learning experience, and monitor the progress and degree of learning. For double-loop learning, chairpersons should encourage teachers to view these four characteristics diagnostically.

The First Class. The opening moments of the first class in a course are critical. Setting the stage for double-loop learning is best done in those opening moments. The first topic should be to describe the new pedagogy. The reasons for altering the classroom format are discussed. An autobiographical approach enhances the message that this course is going to be different.

If it is an interpersonal-skills course, it is emphasized that the real learning of a new behavior takes place at work. Each week, the students will be equipped with a new skill to practice with real colleagues in the work situation. Therefore, the class is to be seen as running for a week, rather than for a session. If it is a theory course, the congruity of theory and practice is emphasized. Each week, the student will be provided a new set of lenses, a new theory, for viewing the world. The students are asked to take that theory into the real world and search for congruity with their behavior in their lives and in their work organizations.

The instructor can expect students to be anxious and resistant to a new pedagogy, particularly one intended to produce double-loop rather than single-loop learning. Resistance is normal when expectations about a course are not met. With the introduction of new rules, the student senses that new responses are going to be required and wonders if this is going to be good or bad. Anxieties about new ways of doing things can be reduced by a detailed review of each aspect of the course. Inviting comments and questions gives students an early signal that learning is a search. When questions come, they are answered, and the questioner is thanked for helping to teach the class.

The course outline is kept for last, because it is familiar and should not be discussed until the stage is set that this course is going to be different. The course outline for an innovative course should be very detailed. It tells how the course is structured and the way the final grade is determined. Each class session is named and dated with the readings or skills for that session. Each session has a home assignment. For instance, the first assignment directs the student to view the workplace as an educational resource: "What are the opportunities to observe theory in practice at your workplace? What are the opportunities to practice new skills in your workplace?" One student convened his subordinates the morning after each class of a management theory course, to discuss the application of the theory of the week. Subordinates saw this as a free course in management theory, taught by their boss. Later, this same student took an interpersonal-skills course. In this case, he convened the same subordinates and asked them to help him learn the new skill of the week. Here, the subordinates were the teachers.

How do the four elements the instructor controls (Ottaway, in press) help one know how to conduct the first class session? The content of the opening class of a course is given, and so the instructor has to use the other three controls to set up the class for double-loop learning. The definition of the task can be raised with the specific instructions of the course outline. In a theory course, the home assignments for checking theory and practice congruity are general, because the material is very single-loop–oriented, and the definition needs to be lowered to enhance a double-loop investigation. In an interpersonal-skills course, suggestions for practicing new skills are very specific, because the material is vague and may be threatening. For example, assignments in a theory course might include the following: "Cite examples of informal groups at work. Are committees and task forces used? What theory, or theories, of motivation are in use at your workplace?" Assignments in an interpersonal-skills course might include the following: "Observe yourself in group settings. Have you increased your power and influence there? Where do you need to improve? Are you noting the behavior of others in your group?"

When the course has been discussed and the course outline and handouts have been distributed, the students introduce each other. The method of introducing students can enhance the double-loop learning possibilities. For instance, the teacher might say, "Now, let's see who we have in the course as resources: learners and fellow teachers. Select someone to interview. Ask why he or she has taken the course. It's okay to say, 'It's the only management elective open on Wednesday night' or 'It's required.' Ask where he or she works. Ask where he or she went to college. Find out what he or she brings to the class and wants to take away from it. Then, reverse the roles and be interviewed. Following this, we will have short introductions of each other." Interviewing should take about five minutes, and then the introductions begin. Having students introduce one another, rather than themselves, is important: This legitimates the sharing of information and the crucial role that fellow students play in the learning process. By now, it is usually midway through the first session. After a break, go right into the first topic of the course.

Journal Keeping. Journal keeping is widely practiced. In courses for part-time students, the journal can be used as Picasso used it—as a workshop (Kakutani, 1986). In the journal, ideas can be shaped and refined. The student has a private place to experiment and practice using new thoughts. Liberties can be taken. Ideas not ready for public practice can be shaped. The student does not have to write perfect sentences or complete a paragraph. The journal is an extension of the mind. About 80 percent of students report journal keeping to be a positive experience.

Whether to grade journals is debatable. The student should be told in the first session if the teacher will see the journals. I prefer that the journal be a private part of the course. The class is asked from time to time if there are problems with the journal. Students will ask questions about the journals, and fellow students seem to be the best resource to answer those questions. Others have experimented with grading journals. Caliguari (1987) claims that grading them increases the volume and quality of the entries. He has students bring the journals to the midterm examination, where he grades them while the students are taking the test.

Journals form the backbone of the part-time pedagogy. They are the mechanism by which the course material gets engaged with the situation back home. They also set up a record of the learning experience, to which the student can return in the future. Journals are not vaults for storing precious or useless artifacts; they are the personal history of one's growth and development. Journals are the basic research tool for integrating new resources into one's life and reflecting on their meaning. I suggest that students select an annual day, such as New Year's Day, to review their journals and plan what to learn next.

An interesting example of the use of journals is in the course "Perspectives on the Individual" at Fairleigh Dickinson University. The course is a series of readings (such as *Brave New World*, *Gilgamesh*, *Civilization and Its Discontents*, *Autobiography of Malcolm X*) and classroom sessions in which the teacher uses the readings to explore perspectives on the individual through group exercises and lectures. Students keep journals of reflections on the connections made among the classroom readings, experiences, and personal life. This is a serious effort to have a double-loop learning experience.

Each assignment has a focus question for students to use. This practice may tend to restrict many students to answering the question in a single-loop way, but is helpful for students who need more structure. Journals are collected weekly. Some professors collect a page from the journal, and others have the students hand in a summary page. These are graded as class participation.

From the viewpoint of the chairperson, this example has two interesting points. One is the teacher's reactions to the use of a journal as part of the class. The curriculum was designed by a committee from all colleges in the university. The use of a journal was hotly debated. Some thought that it would take the focus away from the learnings to be gained from the readings and lectures the teacher would give. Others thought that it would enhance the interaction between the student and the readings. Finally, it was decided to include the journal on a trial basis. After one semester, the teachers were in favor of the journal, because they were impressed with the additional insights they gained about students and their reactions to the readings.

The second point of interest to chairpersons is the student's reaction. The first semester was a struggle between the teachers and students. They sensed that the rules had been changed. They would not have used our language, but they realized that there had been a shift from single-loop learning to double-loop learning. Also, the work load was greater than before, and students were now dealing with professors who were teaching a course and using teaching methods that were determined by many teachers. This was a major cultural change in the life of the university. The first use of an innovative teaching technique is the most resisted. With the faculty working together and persisting, the climate has changed. Students now accept the course, and teachers are more satisfied with their role in it.

Reporting Back. This is a critical step in the process. Here, the students teach one another by going directly to their small groups at the beginning of each class. In the interpersonal-skills classes, these are called the Safe Groups. These groups are composed of a cross-section of the work organizations present. This increases the interest, cuts down on in-talk from one company, and helps each person see that the grass is about the same color in all fields. The groups are balanced in gender, age, and number of full-time students.

Full-time students can present a challenge to this method of teaching. In undergraduate teaching, the disparity of age and experience between full-time and part-time students may be great. This can be a problem in a theory class. When there are several full-time students in a theory class, more control needs to be exercised. The full-time students are spread throughout the groups. They can be made researchers for the group. In this capacity, they monitor the business news for information that the part-time students do not have time to read, or they can look for additional information on topics that interest the group. When there are several full-time students in the class, monitoring the groups more closely ensures that the level of activity is high and well focused. The full-time students can be asked to tell the group what they have learned from part-time students. Full-time students need to feel essential to the learning process in the reporting-back time. Part-time students can adopt full-time students to take them to their workplaces for observation or data collection. Caliguari (1987) sits in on each group each evening, to answer questions and encourage focused activity. Full-time students do not pose a problem in an interpersonal-skills class.

The Safe Group is a very important learning time in the interpersonal-skills courses. Each person, working from the journal, reports his or her efforts to practice the new skill. The other students act as coaches or teachers and give feedback to the reporter. This session reinforces successful efforts to practice the new skill. The supportive environment also makes it a safe place to describe failures. The groups tend to grow very close and to look forward to this time.

After the group has worked for about twenty minutes, a spokesperson from each group tells some of the highlights of the session. This material may prompt the instructor to comment on the reports or add items that were misunderstood or neglected. In the skills course, giving attention to reports that illustrate particularly difficult aspects of skills can be effective. The report period pulls the class together and provides key findings to everyone.

Chairpersons will find that teachers often feel at risk when using groups, because they fear that they waste time. There is that possibility. Some students complain of poor time management. They feel the group time is too long, boring, and too full of gripes or socializing. These are risks. There are several steps the instructor can take to encourage the groups to stay on the topic. One is to walk around the classroom during this time. Another is to intervene when it feels appropriate. Occasionally, a group will ask for help. Teachers can follow the example of Caliguari (1987) and systematically visit each group each session. On the basis of course evaluations that are collected at the end of each course, most students find the groups interesting and helpful.

Analytical Critique. The fourth part of the process is the analytical critique of the whole learning experience. This is where students subject experience to conscious criticism. The critique is handled differently in the theory course and in the interpersonal-skills course. In the theory course, the student writes a critique of the journal. This amounts to a term paper, which counts for a percentage of the final grade. The student is instructed to go over the journal entries and identify what was learned and how. In the theory course, a traditional exam is also given.

In the interpersonal-skills course, the analytical critique has two parts. The first part is a performance evaluation of self and each other person in the Safe Group. The students know that this is expected from the start. One of the early steps in the skills course is the writing of a learning contract by each student. This contract is shared with the other members of the Safe Group, so that everyone can help everyone else learn the skills. For the performance evaluation, the student identifies what was contracted to be learned and makes an evaluation of the degree to which this was accomplished. An entire class period is given to a process where each person hears an evaluation from the other members of the Safe Group. These evaluations are graded.

The second part of the analytical critique for the skills course is a paper identifying when and how the new skills were learned. This is to emphasize that journals are not just records but are to be used to reflect on the whole experience. The exercise also focuses attention on identifying when learning has taken place. This effort emphasizes that learning can occur in the workplace as well as in the classroom.

Summary

This proposed pedagogy for adult part-time learners is intended to generalize the ideas of Argyris and Schön (1974) to all disciplines. This process of presentation, testing in the field, returning for discussion, and analytical critique is intended to increase the congruity of theory and practice in the workplace. This pedagogy also promotes double-loop learning beause of its investigative nature, whereby all are teachers and learners together. Finally, this pedagogy enables learners to be reflective and learn from their learning. The result of such a pedagogy, I am convinced, is a step in the right direction: toward creating effective lifelong learners, a goal of any department and department chairperson.

References

Argyris, C. *Reasoning, Learning, and Action: Individual and Organizational.* San Francisco: Jossey-Bass, 1982.

Argyris, C., and Schön, D. A. *Theory In Practice: Increasing Professional Effectiveness.* San Francisco: Jossey-Bass, 1974.

Caliguari, P. "A User's Perspective of the Pedagogy." Paper presented at Eastern Academy of Management, Boston, May 15, 1987.

Kakutani, M. "Picasso's Documented Interior." *New York Times*, May 26, 1986, p. 28.

Ottaway, R. N. "A Proposed Pedagogy for Management Education of Part-Time Students." *The Organizational Behavior Teaching Review*, 1985, *10*, (2), 71–79.

Ottaway, R. N. "What's the Best Teaching Style?" *Trainer's Workshop*, in press.

Ottinger, C. A. "The Adult Learner: Housewife to Headquarter CEO." In American Council on Education (ed.), *Higher Education Today: Facts in Brief.* Washington, D.C.: American Council on Education, 1987.

Zemke, R., and Zemke, S. "Thirty Things We Know for Sure About Adult Learning." *Training/HRD*, 1981, *18*, 45–52.

Richard N. Ottaway is campus chairperson of the Department of Management and Marketing at the Madison Campus of Fairleigh Dickinson University.

*Programs and practices that enhance the effectiveness of
teaching assistants can have a tremendous impact on the
quality of instruction in a department.*

The Development of TAs:
Preparing for the Future
While Enhancing the Present

Marilla D. Svinicki

Close your eyes and imagine your department with no teaching
assistants. How many additional faculty members would you need to
cover your classes? How many sections would have to be cancelled if
additional instructors could not be hired? Who would monitor those
three-hour labs? What would be the impact on the design of courses, the
learning and morale of the students?

Keller (1986) reports that at some representative California
universities, 30 percent of the classes were taught by teaching assistants
and assistant instructors, a number not out of line with other institutions.
In recent years, departments have become more dependent on graduate
teaching assistants to keep class sizes manageable, and yet these student-
teachers are often the last ones to be considered for professional
development, possibly because of the transient nature of their appoint-
ments. Fortunately for the quality of the undergraduate experience,
institutions are beginning to realize that teaching assistants deserve
preparation for their responsibilities, an attitude encouraged by a recent
national panel on higher education (National Institute of Education,
1984). The purpose of this chapter is to examine what steps the

A. F. Lucas (ed.). *The Department Chairperson's Role in Enhancing College Teaching.*
New Directions for Teaching and Learning, no. 37. San Francisco: Jossey-Bass, Spring 1989.

department chairperson can take to facilitate the development of teaching assistants.

The Teaching Assistant's Role

Before a department can plan for teaching assistants' development, it must make clear for itself and its teaching assistants what their position in the department is and what the assistantship is intended to accomplish. Is it a way of funding graduate study, while getting departmental teaching tasks done? Is it a way of providing undergraduates with small-group educational experiences, which would be prohibitively expensive otherwise? Is it a way of training graduate students for their future professional lives?

Each alternative has implications for the types of programs a department chooses. For example, if very few graduate students in your department actually plan college teaching as a career, it is reasonable for your program to concentrate on equipping them for their immediate tasks only. If many of your graduates will be seeking academic positions, you can strengthen their credentials by using the assistantship as a training period for that aspect of their careers.

Clarifying the purpose of the teaching assistantship also contributes to good working relationships between supervising faculty members and teaching assistants and between teaching assistants and students. New teaching assistants often are unclear about their roles and responsibilities, which leads to apprehension, confusion, and unrealistic expectations in their interactions with supervisors and students. If faculty members in a department differ in their views of the purpose of the teaching assistantship, there could be discrepancies in responsibilities, work loads, and instructor–teaching assistant relationships. Bringing the variety of purposes for the assistantship into the open for discussion, the department enhances the likelihood of recognizing and avoiding problems in the communication of expectations to students and faculty members.

Another aspect of clarifying the teaching assistantship is examining just what assignments the teaching assistants are given and what those assignments require in terms of teaching skills. Teaching assistants assume many roles in different departments, and the type of preparation they require depends on these roles. Figure 1 illustrates how different types of teaching assistant assignments involve different skills.

An irony emerges when one considers this list of skills. We often think that we give teaching assistants the least demanding teaching tasks, when, in reality their assignments can be the most difficult from a teaching perspective. By recognizing the often complex nature of the

Figure 1. Teaching Assistant Assignments and Related Skills

Assignment	Skills Required
Grader: This teaching assistant is responsible for grading the students' work. His or her contact with the students usually is limited to those times when the grading process must be explained or has been challenged.	1. Understand or set the grading criteria and maintain consistency in their application, sometimes coordinating with other graders. 2. Have a grasp sufficient to evaluate answers, the complexity of that depending on the type of answers (machine-scorable versus written responses). 3. Understand and be able to recognize possible cases of academic dishonesty. 4. In some cases, determine the assignment of grades; if not that, understand how student work gets assigned letter grades. 5. Discuss grading procedures and results with the students.
Tutor: The tutor's task is to work on an individual basis with students who have questions about the assignments, the content, the course procedures, and so on.	1. Have a grasp of the content sufficient to assist another individual (usually one with very little background) in understanding complex material. 2. Be able to simplify explanations, make complex concepts more concrete, and rephrase ideas, using different words and examples when the first explanation doesn't work. 3. Be able to ask and answer questions clearly. 4. Be able to probe for and diagnose problems in understanding. 5. Be able to give positive and negative feedback. 6. Build an atmosphere of trust, confidence, and willingness on the part of the students to ask for help. 7. Say no when a student is overdependent or asks for too much help or is simply avoiding working the problem out.
Review section leader: Teaching assistants with this type of assignment work with groups of students to practice skills and answer questions about problem procedures. This type of assignment would be typical of content areas such as math classes, foreign-language classes, and basic-content classes in the sciences.	1. Have many of the same skills of explaining, asking and answering questions, probing for understanding and giving feedback as the tutor. 2. Have many of the same skills of grading assignments and explaining the grading procedures as the grader. 3. Build rapport with the students as a group, so that the students will feel confident enough to participate in class and try the various tasks. 4. Give minilectures to explain procedures and concepts that were not clear in the text or main lectures. 5. Prepare students for upcoming exams and review exam results to clear up problems students may have had.
Discussion leader: This role occurs more in classes where the purpose of the course is to explore ideas and attitudes and where the problems and answers are not straightforward. Examples are literature classes, social science classes, philosophy classes, and the more traditional liberal arts curriculum.	1. Ask and answer questions in a way that focuses attention on the process being followed rather than on the correct answer. 2. Know the content well enough to be able to see it from several points of view and evaluate new perspectives on the spot. 3. Through verbal and nonverbal feedback, direct the flow of the discussion, both in terms of who talks and what is said. 4. Step in when the discussion lags or the students are unprepared and "jump-start" it, which requires a degree of flexibility and originality.

Figure 1. (*continued*)

Assignment	Skills Required
	5. Have enough self-control to allow the students to do the discussing and not to dominate the period.
	6. Highlight main ideas and summarize the discussion periodically, so that the students learn to recognize what is important and what is not.
	7. Evaluate student participation in the discussion for later inclusion in the grade.
Lab section leader: In the sciences, the most common role a teaching assistant will play is that of lab section leader. This involves supervising students as they work individually or in groups in the laboratory setting or on other assignments.	1. Have sufficient content knowledge to ask and answer questions in a variety of different ways to accommodate differences in learner styles.
	2. Be sufficiently familiar with the lab equipment and procedures to do minor troubleshooting and to adapt the procedures when things go wrong. This includes not only experimental procedures but also safety procedures.
	3. Give minilectures, which demonstrate lab procedures or concepts, so that the students can follow those procedures in their own work.
	4. Maintain discipline in the lab and keep the students working on their tasks while assisting students who are having problems.
	5. Evaluate student lab reports—if not for writing style, then at least for accuracy of content.
	6. Monitor for academic dishonesty in lab work and lab reports.
	7. Assign grades that reflect lab reports and in-class performance.

Note: These lists are not intended to be exhaustive, but merely to highlight the wide range of activities required of teaching assistants.

teaching assistant assignment, a department can design development programs that meet the needs of these assignments.

A Policy Handbook

Once a department has a clear notion of its expectations for teaching assistants and how they fit into the overall instructional picture, a useful step is to put those expectations into writing. Examples of teaching assistant handbooks are available from the Educational Research and Information Center (ERIC) in most college and university libraries.

Course Assignment Procedures

It is amazing how many departmental decisions are made for administrative rather than pedagogical reasons. The assignment of teaching assistants is one of these decisions. Teaching assistants are frequently assigned to courses at the last minute, sometimes after classes have begun, with little regard to their preferences and sometimes even without regard to their backgrounds or preparation. This gives them little time to do any thinking about or preparing for teaching tasks. Perhaps the most significant single change a department chairperson could make to improve the performance of teaching assistants would be to make assignments far enough in advance to allow adequate preparation. Encouraging the supervising faculty to inform their assigned teaching assistants of outside readings and other course activities and providing copies of any previous syllabi prior to the semester would also be useful.

In addition to maximizing precourse preparation time, you might want to consider giving some attention to teaching assistants' preferences in their assignments. Teaching assistants who are assigned to courses in their specialty areas or to courses for which they have expressed a preference may be more highly motivated and better prepared. Likewise, assignment to the same course over several semesters would provide some stability to the teaching assistant's life and make the work load less onerous as the semesters progressed. The quality of teaching would improve as the teaching assistant became more comfortable and knowledgeable about the content, the students, and the course procedures.

Supervising Faculty

The success of many teaching assistants depends on supervising faculty members. If supervisors are committed to the notion of the assistantship as a learning opportunity, they can go a long way toward developing graduate students into superior instructors. Faculty members who have teaching assistants for their courses would benefit from some suggestions on supervision. For example, a departmental handbook on that topic might be a useful project for a chairperson to initiate. Such a handbook might contain departmental policies affecting teaching assistants, a summary of the typical teaching assistant assignments and the skills and expectations involved in each, and suggestions for activities that would serve as learning experiences for teaching assistants.

For new faculty members, a presemester meeting on the care and feeding of teaching assistants—led by the more established members of the department, with input from experienced teaching assistants—would be an excellent orientation to these responsibilities.

It would be desirable if the department could provide tangible evidence that the supervision of teaching assistants was valued. For example, work-load credits could be assigned for the supervision of more than two teaching assistants in a given course, just as they are for the supervision of independent graduate work, provided that the instructor engaged in some type of organized activity designed to develop teaching assistants. The opportunity to have teaching assistants assigned to one's course should be recognized as both a benefit and a responsibility. Faculty members who misuse or fail to provide their teaching assistants with adequate supervision and training should be denied their assistance.

Training Programs

More and more institutions are beginning to recognize that teaching does not necessarily come naturally but involves skills and attitudes that can be learned. As a result, they are establishing programs for training teaching assistants in the art and science of teaching.

The Apprentice/Mentor Model. This is the most common form of training to be found. It relies heavily on the supervising professor to provide the teaching assistant with the necessary information, experiences, and feedback to learn the tasks associated with teaching. In the ideal situation, the faculty member recognizes that this is an opportunity for the teaching assistant to learn new skills and to develop new perspectives. To that end, he or she works with the teaching assistant to set goals for the semester, which clarify their respective roles and responsibilities and describe skills that the teaching assistant will develop. They meet regularly to review what is occurring in class, to plan for upcoming classes, and, most significant, to discuss why certain activities are scheduled, why the content is presented as it is, and why certain administrative decisions are made. In addition, the supervising faculty member would arrange for the teaching assistant occasionally to handle other aspects of the course (for example, present a lecture to the class), in order to practice some of these skills and receive feedback on performance.

Organized Meetings. The second most common form of training comes in the form of organized meetings. These meetings are found in situations where several teaching assistants assist in the same course and meet on a regular basis with the supervising faculty member.

While in most cases these meetings are organized to convey course administration information and to solve immediate problems, some planning on the part of the supervisor can make them learning experiences as well. For example, as the course progresses, the supervisor can spend time in the meeting discussing the thinking behind various course decisions and activities, even allowing the teaching assistants to participate in the decision-making process.

Teaching assistants whose responsibilities include preparation of course activities can share and compare activities with the others as another activity in these meetings. This not only distributes the work load but also gives teaching assistants the experience of designing something that can be used by others, as well as of understanding and adapting something that someone else has designed.

Teaching assistants in this situation can be formed into groups in which the members visit one another's classes for the purpose of providing feedback on how the teaching appears to an informed outsider. Members of the group can develop their own questions for observing, focus on particular problems of the moment, and provide encouragement as well as critical feedback. These observations can then be discussed in the meeting, and experiences can be compared.

Presemester Orientations. When teaching assistants are identified early enough to allow it, some departments require attendance at orientation sessions prior to the semester. In recent years, these formerly bureaucratic occasions have begun incorporating discussions about teaching. Only so much can be accomplished in a short time, but an introduction to departmental attitudes toward the importance of teaching and expectations for teaching assistants sets the tone for the semester and provides a foundation on which to build.

Organized Courses. Many institutions have taken the step of offering academic credit in the form of organized courses on teaching for teaching assistants. In some cases, these courses are required before the graduate student can be assigned to a class; in others, they must be taken simultaneously with the first teaching assignment.

The actual content of these courses depends on the department's view of the assistantship, as discussed earlier. A particularly potent component of these courses has been the use of microteaching and feedback. In the microteaching situation, a teaching assistant prepares and teaches several short (ten or fifteen minutes) lessons to his or her fellow teaching assistants and receives suggestions about strengths and ways to improve. The segments are then retaught, and the suggestions are incorporated in subsequent presentations.

Informative Feedback System

Once the teaching assistants have been properly assigned to their courses and provided with a solid foundation for teaching, through seminars and materials, the department should establish an ongoing program of feedback to provide teaching assistants and their supervisors with information about performance in the classroom. There are several alternatives that a department might consider.

A System for Feedback During the Semester. Many programs in faculty development have regular systems for tapping student input while the class is in progress. For example, teaching assistants can work together to visit one another's classes during the semester and gather written feedback from students. The visitor would read over and summarize student comments for the class instructor. The instructor and evaluator then switch roles.

In place of written student feedback, some programs use a technique called small-group instructional diagnosis (Clark and Richmond, 1981), in which a visitor, such as a faculty development consultant or other instructor, interviews the class as a group after they have talked among themselves in small groups. The interviewer then meets with the instructor to discuss what went on and to identify possible changes.

Alternatively, a department might create a short, scaled feedback form, which can be distributed to students and quickly summarized by the teaching assistant. However, more information can be gleaned from the written-response system than through scaled items, especially for the purpose of fine-tuning a course in progress.

A System for End-of-Semester Evaluation. Most institutions now have systems for collecting student evaluations at the end of the semester. Teaching assistants should be encouraged to participate in this system and review the results for improvement purposes.

An important component of each of these feedback systems is the availability of assistance in interpreting and acting on the results. The department should have an experienced faculty member, possibly the supervising professor or a faculty development consultant, review the evaluations with each teaching assistant. The two can plot strategies to improve areas of instruction shown to be weakest and to take advantage of skills the teaching assistant already has.

If no system for collection of such information exists at your institution, your department may want to design one for your own use. There are many models available from a variety of institutions. Again, ERIC is a good source of examples from different institutions and disciplines.

A System for Class Observation and Feedback. An important role that a supervising faculty member can play is that of classroom observer, sitting in on a teaching assistant's class and providing feedback on the session. Postobservation chats about what was seen and what could be done in that particular setting would help the teaching assistant learn from the classroom situation. It may not be practical for the supervising professor to visit classes as often as would be useful for development purposes. In that case, the "buddy" system, as described earlier, can be useful.

The teaching assistant can become his or her own observer by having a class period video- or audiotaped and reviewing the tape later. It would be helpful to provide some information about the kinds of behavior to observe before the tape is reviewed. For example, a teaching assistant might be interested in noting the kinds of questions students ask and how he or she responds to them. The type of behavior observed would depend on the goals of the course and of the teaching assistant. This type of self-monitoring can help the teaching assistant learn to modify his or her own teaching and be more conscious of what is going on in the class, even in the midst of it.

Whatever system of feedback the department uses, an important aspect of it will be the help offered the teaching assistant for interpreting and acting on it. While the department chairperson might not be the best one to handle this task individually, the program should have the backing of the chairperson and be used for rewarding as well as checking on teaching assistants.

Special Needs of International Teaching Assistants

Recently, there has been an increase in international students entering U.S. graduate schools, particularly in the sciences and engineering. Many international students become teaching assistants, a situation that presents chairpersons with both problems and possibilities. A chairperson needs to think carefully about the assignment of international students as teaching assistants in order to minimize the problems of language and culture while maximizing the advantages of having undergraduates interact with these teaching assistants.

The programs already described apply to international teaching assistants as readily as to U.S. teaching assistants, with some important additions. Matching a student's abilities with teaching assistant responsibilities is an important first step. Even if an international teaching assistant is fluent in English, he or she might have problems with some of the most common teaching assignments. The educational systems in some cultures are not as heavily based on inquiry and the questioning of authority as our system is; therefore, discussions among students and the instructor might be very foreign to some teaching assistants. Grading assignments might be more appropriate than in-class assignments for some international teaching assistants whose reading comprehension of English is better than their oral proficiency.

International teaching assistants can compensate for and over-come language barriers when in-class responsibilities are assigned. Helping these teaching assistants to understand the necessity of putting things in writing and providing many channels of information can overcome a lot of the problems.

Providing international teaching assistants with faculty mentors from similar cultural backgrounds, in addition to a supervising instructor, can help ease them over some rough spots. Helping the international teaching assistants build friendships with their American counterparts also provides another source of support and acculturation.

The key is recognizing that language and cultural differences mean international teaching assistants need your special attention when they begin their assignments.

Conclusion

The projects outlined in this chapter are by no means the only things a chairperson can do to develop the teaching capabilities of teaching assistants. These are examples of the type of thinking necessary to design programs to serve that end. There are excellent references on the training of teaching assistants, specifically Andrews (1985) and Chism (1987), which discuss in more detail some of the ideas contained in this chapter and give many examples of programs currently used in a variety of institutions and disciplines.

Whatever program you choose, it is important to recognize the significance of the cadre of teaching assistants who do duty in every department. Theirs is not an easy task, but with the support and encouragement of the department, they can make a significant contribution to the quality of the undergraduate program and will go on to be ambassadors for the department and the profession when they leave to pursue their own careers. Their future is ours as well.

References

Andrews, J.D.W. (ed.). *Strengthening the Teaching Assistant Faculty*. New Directions for Teaching and Learning, no. 22. San Francisco: Jossey-Bass, 1985.

Chism, N. (ed.). *Institutional Responsibilities and Responses in the Employment and Education of Teaching Assistants: Readings from a National Conference*. Columbus: Center for Teaching Excellence, Ohio State University, 1987.

Clark, D. J., and Richmond, M. V. *Small-Group Instructional Diagnosis*. Seattle: Biology Learning Resource Center, University of Washington, 1981.

Keller, S. "Teaching Assistants Get Increased Training." *The Chronicle of Higher Education*, October 29, 1986, pp. 6, 9–10.

National Institute of Education. Study Group on the Conditions of Excellence in American Higher Education. *Involvement in Learning: Realizing the Potential of American Higher Education*. Washington, D.C.: U.S. Department of Education, 1984.

Marilla D. Svinicki is associate director of the Center for Teaching Effectiveness at the University of Texas at Austin. She currently serves as executive director of the Professional and Organizational Development Network in Higher Education.

Some simple devices can give professors surprising
knowledge about how their students learn and about how to
further their learning.

Helping Faculty to Help Their Students Learn

Joseph Katz

The first thing the chairperson should be aware of is that his or her
departmental colleagues are not likely to know very much about how
students learn. We have some sense of what our students do in our
courses. We read their tests and exams. We administer evaluation forms
toward the end of the semester. Students come to us and give us reactions
about our teaching. Gossip provides more or less reliable feedback. Even
if information from these sources were more reliable, however, it would
tell us little about what we need to know most: the process of teaching
and the ways in which our students learn.

How can we obtain that knowledge? I have found that some
simple devices give teachers valuable and sometimes surprisingly
sophisticated information. For instance, we can ask students a few times
during the semester to spend about ten or fifteen minutes to write down
what they are learning in the course and how they are learning it.
Obtaining such feedback during the semester has a great advantage over
end-of-semester evaluations, because what one learns can affect the course
while it is in progress. A colleague of mine asks his students at the end of
the period to sum up what they have learned during the class hour.
Instead of his summing up, as is the custom, he has the students do it as a
means of having them actively reflect on what happened. By reading their

A. F. Lucas (ed.). *The Department Chairperson's Role in Enhancing College Teaching.*
New Directions for Teaching and Learning, no. 37. San Francisco: Jossey-Bass, Spring 1989.

reports, he gains a picture of how the hour appeared to them, rather than to him. Another colleague gives carbon sheets to different students at different times and asks that they be put underneath the sheets on which they are taking notes, for collection at the end of class.

The most effective means I have discovered for obtaining knowledge about how students learn in our courses is a more elaborate procedure. It requires having two faculty members working with each other. One of them selects for study any course he or she is currently teaching. The other serves as an observer or coinquirer but does not coteach. The observer comes to class at regular intervals. Observations do not by themselves tell us very much, because they do not give us knowledge about what goes on in the minds of the students. Hence, both the teacher and the observer interview students on a regular basis. Each of them selects about three students whom they interview throughout the semester.

The interviews focus not on the teacher but on the students and their ways of learning. Questions are asked, such as why the students picked the course, what they expected and what they are getting, how they go about reading the assignments and preparing for class, how they prepare for tests and exams, and how they would describe the class process and the students' and the teacher's parts in it. These interviews, if conducted in an open-ended and inquiry-oriented way, yield detailed information about how the students conceive the subject matter of the course and about how they respond to and cope with it. Such data show us where students are heading in terms of their own motivation, as well as ways in which the materials of the course can be brought more in touch with what makes students curious. Environmental and psychological factors that keep students from using or developing their cognitive capacities can also be identified.

The teacher and the observing colleague meet for about an hour, preferably once a week, to discuss what they have learned from their interviews and observations of students. The reflections during these meetings almost immediately lead the teacher to make modifications in methods of interacting with the class and thus engender an ongoing experimentation, the results of which can be checked immediately in the observations and interviews.

Thus far it may seem as if students are viewed primarily as objects for study. However, in recent years, learning as collaboration has become an acceptable model. In this view of learning, students are coinquirers with their teachers. The teacher is a mature guide who realizes that only what students learn on their own will become part of their mental equipment. Using such a model as a base, even testing and grading can take on a more collaborative nature. Interviews with students become occasions when, helped by the interviewer's questions and encouraging presence, students investigate how they are learning—knowledge that will be useful to them in guiding their own intellectual evolution.

Occasionally an entire class can be drawn into this process: Teachers may devote part or all of a class period to exploring with students how they are going about learning in the course. One can ask them such questions as what they think about the contents of the course and its epistemology or about how data are collected and reflected on in the subject under study. One can ask questions about the classroom process, the readings, the tests and papers, and what the students find helpful and not so helpful for their own learning. The observing colleague can be present, too, and can contribute to the exploration.

The interviews and the group sessions serve the purpose of what some people call *metacognition.* The students' growing awareness of the ways in which they learn helps them to develop more effective ways of studying. Almost inevitably, this approach leads students and faculty toward a more inquiry-oriented approach, instead of one that relies on the transmission of facts. The latter mode is still the predominant one; lecturing is by far the method of choice in most classes, even in small classes. Even when teachers' intent is to stress critical thinking, their actual procedures (as revealed, for instance, by their exam questions) often revert to the information-transmitting mode. It takes some learning on the part of teachers to shed the preconception that students learn when teachers talk and to move toward procedures that allow students to be actively involved.

An example from mathematics, a field thought to be particularly resistant to an inquiry approach, will provide an illustration. Professor Alvin White, in teaching his introductory course at Harvey Mudd College, has his students consult not one but several textbooks. He asks them to read at least two texts in any specific problem area.. These texts reveal different approaches to the same subject matter and hence require students to reflect on the discrepancies and identify problems as they view them. Professor White divides his class into two or three teams. Each is given or asked to pose two problems, one solvable and the other one unsolvable. The teams compete in a productive and playful manner with each other, sometimes discovering solutions to the unsolvable problem. Prizes or other recognition are occasionally given to the winning team.

Another of White's practices is to have lunch with his students at regular intervals. The topics of conversation range all the way from gossip about mathematics and mathematicians to reflections on the philosophy of mathematics, thus mirroring the kinds of talk that professionals engage in at meetings of their professional associations and on other occasions. It makes clear to the students how human an enterprise mathematics is, and it makes it much less forbidding and more personal. Even more important, these lunches give the professor a sense of students' perceptions, so that his interactions with them in the classroom can be more fully responsive to their ways and quirks of thinking and, at least in some fashion, to their personalities.

There are other ways in which students can be encouraged to approach their courses in an inquiry-oriented mode. Relating course-work to out-of-classroom data gathering (for example, obtaining oral histories) or to experiences in the field or inservice activities, using students' job experiences as subjects of investigation, having students work on projects as teams, having students discuss one another's papers or even exams—all these encourage the students to use and develop their own critical, imaginative, and theory-building skills. The classroom itself becomes an investigative laboratory. Even in large lecture classes, the teacher can divide the class into smaller groups and ask them to discuss the ideas and the texts of the course.

The practices described here are not prescriptive blueprints but rather examples to free our minds to larger possibilities of obtaining knowledge about how our students learn and how to further their learning. The department chairperson can be knowledgeable about these ideas and may want to put together a library for faculty in order to encourage active reflection about teaching.

One of the most important things that chairpersons can do is to make it possible for their departmental colleagues to experiment. My own studies have given me some indication that many more faculty are ready for educational experimentation than will openly admit it. Faculty fear that an experiment will lead to lower student evaluations or other negative reactions (as in fact may happen). It is important for chairpersons to let department colleagues know that educational experimentation is valued, even though results may not be the anticipated or desired ones. Actually, the possibility of failure is often exaggerated.

Another way in which chairpersons can play a crucial role is in establishing a context for talking about teaching. Even in strongly teaching-oriented institutions, it is uncommon for faculty to engage in much talk about their teaching. One can only speculate about the causes of this reluctance. One of my suspicions is that because teaching is so important to so many of us, and because our sense of self depends so much on its success, we are reluctant to talk to others for fear of exhibiting weaknesses and, perhaps, fantasies that we do not care to expose to others. The cure for that reluctance is to talk about teaching on a regular and professional basis. Groups of faculty need to be encouraged to get together to submit teaching—or better, student learning—to sustained analysis. One might begin with descriptions (perhaps videotapes) of teaching in other institutions and move toward an examination of one's own classrooms. Such group sessions may include only members of one department, but it will often be desirable to form such groups across departmental lines, with perhaps only one or two members of a department participating. This would get around reluctance engendered by closeness to one's colleagues or by department politics. The chairpersons of several departments, working together, could play a productive role in facilitating such meetings.

It is desirable that chairpersons subject their own classes to scrutiny. They may choose the methods just described or others, but unless they gain a more vivid picture of how their students go about learning in their classes, they will be less able to guide their colleagues. Some chairpersons may prefer to seek colleagues in other departments and have them visit their classes and interview students.

Good educational thinking and planning require transcending departmental confines. To have our students achieve reasonable competencies by the time they graduate calls for the coordination of the curriculum and for collaboration among teachers. Chairpersons can play an important role in furthering such concerted planning. They can encourage a new spirit of pedagogical vitality. Periodic and articulate discussions and analyses of faculty's work as teachers and their students' ways of learning constitute one approach to revitalizing a department.

In addition, chairpersons can encourage faculty to move beyond their specialties. As disciplines have become more specialized, faculty have avoided teaching courses in areas in which they do not have expert knowledge; yet, most of our lives, we are challenged to use whatever knowledge we have, most of which is not expert. Such knowledge is called *general education*. Chairpersons might encourage faculty to teach courses outside their areas of expertise. It would not only extend their intellectual horizons but also might vivify their disciplinary knowledge from fresh perspectives. Faculty would be more like students when they inquired into areas in which they were not fully expert. They would become more knowledgeable coinquirers with their students, showing students how they go about learning, rather than dispensing familiar knowledge. I also can imagine some wonderful departmental discussions about the history and the epistemology of the discipline, subjecting the discipline to critical inquiry with regard to the questions it raises and how it goes about answering them. Our students, who sometimes ask "the emperor has no clothes" questions, are in a good position to help us.

To talk about teaching at the college level almost inevitably raises the question of the relationship of research to teaching. People often respond to this question in very general ways, ranging from the assertion that research vivifies teaching to the opposite one—that it makes teaching worse because of the overspecialization of the researcher. This question must be answered in much finer detail. Research valuable for a senior seminar may not be so valuable for an introductory course. Specialized research will not help faculty who need to teach the broader dimensions of their fields to undergraduates. Scholarly publication does not necessarily guarantee the ability to communicate with students.

At the same time, many faculty will want to do research—good research. Here, we too often leave them to lonely struggles. Chairpersons may think of ways in which faculty from within and outside their departments can affiliate with each other and form small groups working collaboratively. Such groups would function as think tanks: professors discussing their research questions with one another, offering critiques and suggestions. It would make research much less lonely. This collaboration would extend beyond the substance of research and into how to do it (including how to write). Like students, many faculty procrastinate and become obsessive in their research. Sometimes, rather than their own inclinations, they follow some mandate perceived in graduate school; hence, their research is rather sterile, because it does not express their own voice or inclinations. Chairpersons might seek means for faculty to receive help from one another (or from professionals) to deal with procrastination, obsession, and wrongly perceived mandates.

We might even raise the question of the utility of some or much of the research: How productive is it? How repetitive? We may raise the question of quantity versus quality. Increasingly, the number of publications is the criterion of success. Is it not possible to conceive that lower quantity may mean higher quality, with more of the right questions being asked (and at some leisure), leading to ripening and greater sophistication of ideas?

One of the particularly disconcerting problems that many chairpersons face is the presence of ineffective, alienated, or burned-out colleagues in their midst. It takes a long time for faculty to arrive at that state. We should think more about prevention than about the treatment of casualties. Nevertheless, there are many casualties in our midst. Each case is different; for effective action, one should develop a history and a diagnosis. For instance, there are teachers who are intent on prodding their students toward better performance, and they do so by making provocative remarks, which their students perceive as sarcastic or otherwise hurtful. Such teachers often are not aware of this perception. Over the years, a vicious cycle ensues. Students become more alienated, and the faculty member becomes more rejecting or withdrawn. Such teachers acquire bad reputations in the student grapevine. A bad reputation reaches colleagues and administrators, and such faculty are perceived as a burden. They are treated differently and are not subject to the usual rewards. The vicious cycle continues.

Experience has shown reversals of this pattern, if faculty classified as "dead wood" are given responsibilities that go counter to the reputations they have acquired. Such responsibilities can consist of important committee assignments or other tasks usually reserved for well-regarded faculty. A colleague of mine has recently worked with a highly unpopular fellow faculty member, providing him the opportunity to talk about his relations with the students in his classroom. In a series of interviews, my colleague was able gently to point out the difference between how the faculty member perceived what he was doing and how students perceived his actions and remarks. He became conscious of his sarcastic and belittling behavior, and, as he changed his ways, his students became responsive to him. In general, once faculty members experience approbation from their students, important changes in their feelings and behavior take place.

The procedure sketched earlier in this chapter, in which two faculty members collaborate with each other in observing a course, may be a device that chairpersons would want to use with faculty members who are perceived as not being very successful with their students. Such a faculty member could either be observed or be an observer. In either case, he or she would be able to increase sophisticated reflection about how one works with students. The relationship of the two faculty members would be an important ingredient in overcoming isolation.

It takes many years to arrive at the stage of being alienated and burned out. The faculty member's original interest in a field may have waned, partly because of familiarity and partly because of failure in the kind of scholarship he or she thinks the field requires. A deadening effect may ensue from the fact that one teaches the subject to students who are forever at the elementary level. A new cycle begins with each new group of students, who may never reach the point of discourse at a level at which the professor would like to talk.

There are periods in many faculty lives when satisfaction with teaching is not very strong. The desire to teach may return, if conditions are right. Here is another challenge to the chairperson for prevention and treatment. Faculty may rekindle their excitement in subject matter if they have opportunities for cultivating their intellectual interests—for instance, by spending a semester or two at a research university or by participating in workshops of some duration in areas of present or potential interest. When a faculty member pursues a line of investigation, either within the original field or outside it, the ensuing vitality often spills over to engender a new liveliness in teaching.

Some faculty need time outside academia—sometimes for one or several summers, sometimes for longer periods. Helping faculty find positions in government, industry, or business can lead them to find new careers or to come back invigorated by the experience and incorporate it into their work in the classroom.

The chairperson can do much by devising opportunities for faculty members to meet with one another around areas of common interest—some intellectual, some social, or a combination of both—at monthly wine-and-cheese parties devoted to talking about teaching. It is amazing how apart from each other faculty can live, even faculty in small institutions. They may have rather stereotypical and even not so benign views of one another. By contrast, the energizing effect of faculty talking with each other cannot be overstated. Faculty, of course, do meet around administrative tasks, but these are often turf-minded occasions. The talking together I have in mind is sharing ideas and interests, which will help overcome the inhibitions of talking about teaching and one's own classroom. The creation of such a community is one of the noblest and most practical of the chairperson's tasks.

Joseph Katz is senior fellow at the Woodrow Wilson
National Fellowship Foundation in Princeton, New Jersey.
He is the editor of Teaching as Though Students Mattered
(Jossey-Bass, 1985) and the author, with M. Henry, of
Turning Professors into Teachers *(Macmillan, 1988).*

Student evaluations are most valuable when used to improve teaching.

Using Student Feedback to Improve Teaching

Peter Seldin

Whether we like it or not, students are the only daily observers of their professors' classroom performance. Students are thus one potentially invaluable source of information about their professors' teaching.

Why is there the need for such judgmental information? Two reasons predominate: first, to improve teaching performance and, second, to aid administrative decisions. This chapter will focus on the use of student evaluation for improving teaching.

Actually, there is no greater purpose for evaluation than to improve performance. College and university professors are hired with the expectation that they eventually will be effective teachers. The systematic evaluation of teachers by their students is a logical extension of this expectation. If students need feedback to correct learning errors, faculty members also need feedback to correct teaching mistakes. No matter how good a particular teacher is in the classroom or laboratory, he or she can improve. No matter how effective a particular teaching method is, it can be enhanced. Consider these as postulates in education.

A note of caution is in order. Without a doubt, student assessment is an important component of evaluating teaching performance, but student evaluation by itself is only part of the whole. The proper weight must be accorded to other sources, such as classroom observation,

A. F. Lucas (ed.). *The Department Chairperson's Role in Enhancing College Teaching.*
New Directions for Teaching and Learning, no. 37. San Francisco: Jossey-Bass, Spring 1989.

self-appraisal, samples of instructional material, and videotaped class-room sessions. Despite the clear value of using multiple sources of information, student feedback is the most widely used (and, in many cases, the only) source of information on classroom teaching today (Seldin, 1988).

The value of student evaluation depends in large measure on whether appropriate questions are asked. Students are in a good position to describe or judge such things as the teacher's ability to communicate at their level, the teacher's professional and ethical behavior in the classroom, student-teacher relationships, what has been learned in the course, and how much interest in the subject was stimulated by the teacher. Students are not in a good position to judge the relevance or recency of course content, the knowledge and scholarship of the teacher, or the appropriateness of instructional objectives. These judgments require more professional background and are best left to the teacher's colleagues.

Student Ratings

Student opinions about a professor's classroom teaching can be obtained in many ways. In practice, however, a written questionnaire or rating scale routinely serves the purpose.

Choosing an Instrument. Diagnostic questions, which ask for perceptions or evaluations of specific teaching behaviors and specific aspects of the course, are likely to be more fruitful than general questions about overall teaching effectiveness. The questions should spotlight particular teaching behaviors ("Does the professor vary the speed and tone of his or her voice?") and course characteristics ("Is the assigned reading too difficult?"). The questions should be presented, of course, on a scale and should not call for a *yes* or *no* response. To ask for a *yes* or *no* would not yield the specificity essential to improvement of teaching.

When is it best to issue rating forms to students—early in the term, or at the end? Experience suggests four to six weeks into the term. The reason for such timing is that the professor's performance can then be monitored and deficiencies can be corrected, so that current students are the beneficiaries.

Student ratings can also be a valuable additional source of information in making personnel decisions. If used for that purpose, a short form—probably four to six items—would be sufficient. The questions would be global or overall, rather than diagnostic. The rating form would be administered in the last two weeks of the term, and the results would not be given to the instructor until after the issuance of final grades. Clearly, the purpose of the student rating program determines the kinds of questions asked, when the evaluation is conducted, and when the results are returned to the instructor.

A rating scale should include several items from each of the following:

- *Rapport:* "The instructor is friendly."
- *Work load:* "The instructor asks for too much work."
- *Feedback:* "Tests and papers are graded and returned promptly."
- *Structure:* "The instructor plans class activities in detail."
- *Impact on students:* "My interest in the subject is stimulated by this instructor."
- *Group interaction:* "Students discuss one another's ideas."

Be sure to include some open-ended questions, to allow students to respond more expansively and in their own words: "If you were teaching this course, what is the first thing you would change?" "What are the three traits you liked most about the instructor?" "What was the most significant aspect of this course for you?" "How could the instructor improve as a teacher?"

Weimer (1987b) believes that students should be asked questions that are open yet focused: "When did you find the instructor most or least helpful in your learning?" "When did you feel most or least stimulated by this course?" "Which assignments were most or least relevant to course objectives and student needs?" Questions like these permit students to comment freely yet encourage them to focus on specific instructional aspects, which in turn gives a professor a clearer sense of the instructional strategies or policies needing change—for example, topics requiring greater clarity of presentation.

Braskamp, Brandenberg, and Ory (1984) suggest an innovative strategy for eliciting student opinions about courses and instructors. Students are asked to write one-page mock letters to fellow students who are interested in taking the same course with the same instructor the next semester. In the letters, the students comment on particular aspects of the course and the instructor and conclude with recommendations to enroll in or avoid the course or the instructor.

A word about confidentiality: Student evaluations, when gathered for improvement purposes, must remain confidential. If an evaluation is disclosed to a third party, it must be with the prior consent and at the sole discretion of the evaluated professor. To betray confidentiality is to court institutionwide disaster.

Effects of Student or Instructor Characteristics. Generally speaking, factors that might be expected to influence student ratings have scant or no effect. No consistent relationship has been uncovered between student ratings and the instructor's rank, sex, or research productivity (McKeachie, 1979; Aleomoni and Hexner, 1980; Lowman, 1984; Seldin, 1987). There appears to be no significant link between the amount of assigned work or grading standards and student ratings (Lowman, 1984).

Further, little or no relationship has been found between students' age, sex, year in college, or grade point average and their ratings of instructors (Seldin, 1980; Millman, 1981; Braskamp, Brandenberg, and Ory, 1984; Marsh, 1984). Ratings are marginally higher in small classes (under thirteen students), discussion classes, and classes in the humanities, but the differences are not statistically significant (Braskamp, Brandenberg, and Ory, 1984; Seldin, 1987).

Even when significant relationships between extraneous variables and student ratings are obtained, they account for only 12 to 14 percent of the variance between positive and negative ratings (Marsh, 1984; Seldin, 1987). To put it another way, 86 to 88 percent of the variance between positive and negative student ratings cannot be attributed to extraneous variables.

The Need for Consultation. Will the use of student ratings automatically lead to improved teaching? For most professors, it probably will not. In fact, low ratings and critical student comments can easily lead to anxiety, discouragement, and loss of enthusiasm. Simply giving the diagnosis of classroom problems is not enough; instructors must also be given remedies for the problems. Improved performance is much more likely if ratings are discussed with a professor by a sympathetic and knowledgeable colleague or teaching-improvement specialist, who helps interpret the scores, provides encouragement, and suggests specific teaching-improvement strategies (Cohen, 1980; Aleomoni and Stevens, 1983; Menges and Binko, 1986; Seldin, 1988).

Personal Teaching-Improvement Guides. One telling criticism of student evaluation of teaching performance is that too often it fails to improve performance. Wilson (1987) reports that the University of California at Berkeley has developed an inexpensive yet effective remedy. Called Personal Teaching-Improvement Guides, they are tailored to the needs of individual faculty members. The guides use a twenty-four-item student evaluation form as a starting point. They include very specific descriptions of successful teaching practices, matched to the instructor's lowest-rated items. Thus, faculty members are supplied with simple, proved, practical suggestions that can be used immediately to improve their teaching.

The following are steps for implementing the Personal Teaching-Improvement Guides program.

1. Interested faculty members volunteer to participate in the project.

2. Questionnaires are administered in the classes of participating instructors. The questionnaires contain twenty-four statements probing particular teaching tasks. The students are asked to rate the instructor for each task.

3. Individual teacher-description profiles are generated. They

summarize and display the means, standard deviations, and frequency distributions of students' descriptions of classroom teaching.

4. The profiles are examined and marked by a teaching-improvement specialist who mediates between the raw data from students and the faculty members who are the potential actors in making changes.

5. Personal Teaching-Improvement Guides are assembled for individual professors by careful selection of teaching-improvement packets that address their lowest-rated questionnaire items. There is a teaching-improvement packet for each of the twenty-four statements in the student questionnaire.

6. The personalized guides are distributed to professors during the second week of the following academic term.

7. Professors incorporate into classroom teaching the recommendations in the guides.

8. Professors report on their use of and satisfaction with the guides at the end of the term (Wilson, 1987).

Guidelines for Using Student Ratings

Although student ratings of teachers have been the eye of the storm for over two decades, their worth has now been clearly established. The experience of those years has demonstrated the wisdom of following guidelines and strategies:

1. Place all improvement activities under the instructor's control. Allow the instructor to select the method of student feedback and to target the areas of improvement.

2. Use multiple sources of information. Student ratings should never be the only yardstick for teaching evaluation.

3. Ask diagnostic questions to bring out good descriptions and evaluations of particular teaching behaviors and particular aspects of the course. Ask students only appropriate questions.

4. Encourage professors to comment on student ratings in the context of their teaching methods and goals. Encourage them to supply two or three extra questions to the rating form that are tied to their teaching methods or objectives.

5. Encourage written student comments about particular aspects of the course or teaching strategy. Used in conjunction with diagnostic questions, they are especially useful.

6. Evaluate continuously. To improve their teaching, instructors need a clear record of where they have been and how they are progressing. Since teaching improvement is often painstakingly slow, continuous progress checks are needed to justify the substantial time and effort invested in behavior modification.

7. Provide student rating results only to the evaluated instructor and to no one else without that instructor's consent.

8. Give instructors an interpretive manual containing the norms (average scores, percentiles, and so forth). This makes performance comparison possible. If the norm is compatible with the characteristics of a particular course (for example, a small, upper-level discussion class), the instructor will be able to make much more sense out of the student ratings.

9. Offer professors guidance on strategies for improving teaching. Perhaps a handful of professors can improve on their own after studying their student evaluations. Most professors need private discussions with sympathetic, knowledgeable colleagues who offer counsel and encouragement to change.

Three More Ways to Obtain Information

Although questionnaires and rating forms are the most popular methods of obtaining student feedback on teaching, three other methods are readily available—interviews, small-group instructional diagnosis, and student evaluation committees.

Interviews. The class interview begins with a written request from the professor for an instructional consultant to conduct an interview with the class. The professor arms the consultant with a list of questions or concerns. During the thirty-minute class interview, the students are asked to indicate (by discussion and a show of hands) whether they agree with, disagree with, or feel neutral about each concern. The results are recorded—for example, "Students would like more class discussion: 75 percent agree, 15 percent disagree, 10 percent are neutral." After the interview, the consultant writes a report on the issues discussed, response percentages, and student comments. Finally, the consultant sits down with the professor, discusses the results, and establishes the needed objectives and strategies for improving classroom instruction (Kyger, 1984; Seldin, 1988).

Small-Group Instructional Diagnoses. Here, an instructional consultant or specially trained senior faculty member is invited by the professor to the classroom, usually at the midsemester point. The professor leaves, and the consultant divides the students into groups. Each group is given about ten minutes to reach consensus on three questions: "What do you like about the course?" "What improvements do you think can be made?" "What strategies do you suggest for producing these improvements?" The last question is particularly important, since it confronts the students with the realization that some changes may be difficult, if not impossible.

The consultant records each group's responses, clarifying them if necessary. The responses are summarized and discussed with the professor (Sorcinelli, 1986). The professor is the beneficiary of perceptive and interpretive comments and counsel on remedial strategies. Some professors take the process one step further, by discussing the results with the class. Taking the extra step enables the professor to respond to criticisms and to demonstrate to the students that their views are taken seriously.

Student Evaluation Committees. In this procedure, a small student group (three to five) forms an evaluation committee for the class. Some professors substitute service on the committee for one or more class assignments. The committee meets regularly outside of class to discuss such things as clarity of course objectives, work load, appropriateness of assignments, and teaching style. Input from the rest of the class is encouraged by formal or informal means. The committee meets now and then with the professor during the semester to present its findings (Fuhrman and Grasha, 1983).

The Role of the Department Chairperson

It can be argued that a prime function of the department chairperson is to foster continuing teaching improvement in the department. To some extent, chairpersons accomplish this by serving as role models. A chairperson devoting time and energy to strengthen his or her own teaching, for example, encourages emulations, but chairpersons do more than serve as role models. They create and support the department's "academic culture" (Irvine, 1987). What is academic culture? It is an unspoken language that conveys to faculty members what is considered important and how they are expected to do things in the department.

Seldin (1988) finds that teaching improvement is much more likely when the department's academic culture is marked by a high level of mutual trust and respect between the chairperson and faculty members; a recognition, with no reservations on the part of the chairperson, of the value of appraisal in strengthening performance; clear expectations that the chairperson and the faculty will pursue excellence and will not be satisfied with mediocre performance; adequate resources and consultative support; and performance appraisals based on multiple information sources and firsthand knowledge and characterized by fairness and thoroughness.

How does the chairperson talk with faculty members about improving their teaching skills? Most important, perhaps, is that the chairperson include praise for faculty members' achievements. Since teaching demands a monumental investment of self, it predisposes professors to sensitivity toward criticism. Thus, it is critically important that teaching weaknesses be discussed in a framework of appreciation. The challenge to the chairperson is to accomplish change without disturbing professors' integrity and self-esteem.

Weimer (1987a) suggests that this challenge be met by adopting certain strategies:

1. Focus discussion on teaching behaviors. Avoid dealing with teaching in the abstract. Talk about what effective or ineffective teachers do and do not do.

2. Deemphasize strong judgmental conclusions. The discussion about teaching should focus on instruction, not on evaluation. Recognize that the effects of instruction will vary from one student to another.

3. Present carefully confined conclusions about teaching effectiveness. Make the comprehensiveness of the conclusions consistent with the data on hand. Do not borrow student ratings from one course, for example, and apply them to other courses.

4. Concentrate on motivation to improve and encourage faculty commitment to instruction. Propose ways of being more effective. Offer alternatives. Encourage faculty participation in teaching-development activities.

Good teaching does not just happen; it is the end product of hard work over many years. This long-term commitment to teaching excellence should be the hallmark of all department chairpersons and faculty members.

References

Aleamoni, L. M., and Hexner, P. Z. "A Review of the Research on Student Evaluation and a Report on the Effect of Different Sets of Instructions on Student Course and Instructor Evaluation." *Instructional Science*, 1980, *9*, 67–84.

Aleamoni, L. M., and Stevens, J. J. "The Effectiveness of Consultation in Support of Student Evaluation Feedback: A Ten Year Follow-Up." Tucson: University of Arizona, 1983.

Braskamp, L. A., Brandenberg, D. C., and Ory, J. C. *Evaluating Teaching Effectiveness: A Practical Guide.* Newbury Park, Calif.: Sage, 1984.

Cohen, P. A. "Effectiveness of Student Rating Feedback for Improving College Instruction: A Metaanalysis of Findings." *Research in Higher Education*, 1980, *13*, 321–341.

Fuhrman, B. S., and Grasha, A. F. *A Practical Handbook for College Teachers.* Boston: Little, Brown, 1983.

Irvine, P. "Collegiate Cultures." Paper presented at the Conference on Academic Chairpersons, Orlando, Florida, February 1987.

Kyger, B. L. "Using a Class Interview as a Formative Evaluation Technique." *The Journal of Staff, Program, and Organizational Development*, 1984, *2*, 97–99.

Lowman, J. *Mastering the Techniques of Teaching.* San Francisco: Jossey-Bass, 1984.

McKeachie, W. J. "Student Ratings of Faculty: A Reprise," *Academe*, 1979, *65*, 384–397.

Marsh, H. W. "Students' Evaluations of University Teaching: Dimensionality, Reliability, Validity, Potential Biases, and Utility." *Journal of Educational Psychology*, 1984, *76*, 707–754.

Menges, R. J., and Binko, K. T. "Effects of Student Evaluation Feedback: A Metaanalysis of Higher Education Research." Paper presented at the annual meeting of the American Educational Research Association, San Francisco, April 1986.

Millman, J. (ed.). *Handbook of Teacher Evaluation*. Newbury Park., Calif.: Sage, 1981.

Seldin, P. *Successful Faculty Evaluation Programs*. Crugers, N.Y.: Coventry Press, 1980.

Seldin, P. "Q & A—Evaluating Teaching Performance: Answers to Common Questions." *AAHE Bulletin*, 1987, *40* (1), 9–12.

Seldin, P. "Evaluating and Developing Teaching Performance." Workshop presented at the National Technical Institute for the Deaf, Rochester, New York, April 1988.

Sorcinelli, M. D. *Evaluation of Teaching Handbook*. Bloomington: Dean of Faculties Office, University of Indiana, 1986.

Weimer, M. G. "How to 'Talk' with Faculty Members About Improving Teaching Skills." Workshop presented at the Conference on Academic Chairpersons, Orlando, Florida, February 1987a.

Weimer, M. G. "Open-Ended Questions and Instructional Evaluation." *The Teaching Professor*, 1987b, *1* (10), 7.

Wilson, R. C. *The Personal Teaching-Improvement Guides Program—A User's Manual*. Berkeley: Office of Research on Teaching Improvement and Evaluation, University of California, 1987.

Peter Seldin is professor of management at Pace University in Pleasantville, New York, and has consulted widely on faculty and administrator evaluation and development. He is the author of Changing Practices in Faculty Evaluation *(Jossey-Bass, 1984), and most recently of* Evaluating and Developing Administrative Performance *(Jossey-Bass, 1988).*

*College teaching can be greatly improved and enriched if
chairpersons take the lead in creating a sense of community
and common cause among colleagues.*

The Chairperson
and Teaching

Kerry A. Trask

The quality of teaching in American higher education has been found
wanting by a number of recent reports. The slipping status of the United
States in the world has been blamed, in part, on the inadequate classroom
performances of the country's professors. One of the most severe critics
has been former Secretary of Education William Bennett (1986), who
asserts, "There is an extraordinary gap between the rhetoric and the
reality of American higher education" (p. 28). He charges that there is too
much poor teaching, too little concern for the intellectual growth of
students, and a "collective loss of nerve and faith" among faculty
members and administrators of too many of the nation's universities
(Bennett, 1984, p. 16). Bennett is by no means alone. Others also have
blasted the work being done by college teachers. Newman (1985, p. 23)
has concluded: "College education is nowhere near as exciting or as
effective as it could be. In many ways it is boring, particularly the
classroom part."

Being boring was the one offense for which the dying Roman
writer Seneca could not forgive Nero, and for some of us it is the
comment on student evaluations that cuts the deepest. Sooner or later, it
will be there for all of us, boldly and anonymously pressed down through
four color-coded copies. Our first reaction is likely to be an angry

A. F. Lucas (ed.). *The Department Chairperson's Role in Enhancing College Teaching.*
New Directions for Teaching and Learning, no. 37. San Francisco: Jossey-Bass, Spring 1989.

indignation, hurled back at all those apathetic students who have had the nerve to sit indifferently through some of our very best efforts. But annoyance is mixed with self-doubt and anxiety. At least that was my reaction the first time I read that comment while sitting alone in my office and leafing through the pages I had hoped would reassure me of my effectiveness as a teacher. After that, none of the praise was enough.

Questions about teaching effectiveness, especially our own, are often answered with denials and rationalizations. There is a tendency to respond with standard complaints about dull and unmotivated students, the epidemic spread of cultural illiteracy, and the stingy doling out of funds and recognition by those in power. The claim is frequently made that we do not even really know what good teaching is. Nevertheless, while we may find it difficult to agree about what is good, almost none of us will mistake poor teaching when we see it, and most of us even concur with Bennett's description of it: "Although it can take many forms," writes Bennett (1984, p. 16), poor teaching is "lifeless and tedious, mechanical and ideological," "lacking in conviction," and "perhaps most commonly, it fails to have a sense of the significance of the material it purports to study and teach. . . .It can bore and deaden where it means to quicken and elevate."

There are those who have deep misgivings about whether the ways in which we and others teach can be changed. How we teach is primarily a reflection of personality, asserts a distinguished professor of history, who also points out that "a professor who is dull and plodding in daily life cannot become transformed into a spellbinder in the lecture hall, no matter how carefully he reviews his notes or prepares his outlines." Then, in a note of virtual resignation, Hamerow (1987, p. 153) concludes that "since there is little we can do to change what we are, there is little we can do to change how we teach."

There are still others who, even if willing to suggest that something can be done to change the ways people teach, are deeply disturbed by what they see as an abysmal lack of incentive to do so. Most of the recent reports (and much of the common knowledge within the profession) reveal that academic reward systems do not really have much to offer good teachers. They indicate that the academic profession is deeply divided in its priorities and values. Faculty members are told that good teaching is important, but it is the publishing scholars who are seen (and who see themselves) as the laudable reflections of the proper academic work ethic, while colleagues who concentrate mostly on students and teaching are regarded as unambitious throwbacks to the quaint and leisurely era of Mr. Chips. Research is where the prestige is, and publication is the only sure path to tenure and promotion. Teaching, even excellent teaching, is not enough to ensure professional survival. It may even be held against you. Unfortunately, such conditions are prevalent and certainly have contributed to what is believed to be a widespread deterioration of good teaching.

That decline has produced a sense of crisis and urgent calls for immediate action. There have been some excellent, even inspiring, responses in an outpouring of literature that surpasses anything in higher education since the Progressive Movement at the beginning of this century. Constructive strategies have been devised for improving teaching techniques, especially for involving students much more actively in the learning process, and reforms aimed at the intellectual enrichment of the curriculum have already been implemented. Unfortunately, not all professors have been receptive to these new ideas and methods. Furthermore, technique alone cannot address the deeper problem that Handlin (1979, pp. 4-6) identifies with the tragic loss of the "feeling of community which had sustained and nurtured the profession in the past."

There is much to suggest that Handlin is right. In many colleges and universities, far too many faculty members seem to be in business for themselves—coming and going almost unnoticed, always in a hurry, grudgingly keeping a few office hours, conducting classes almost secretively behind closed doors, and coming in contact with their students only incidentally on their way through. It is not that most professors dislike teaching or students; it is just difficult to find the time. Perhaps that is a sad symptom of the age in which we live, which, when compounded by professional pressures, drives us all deeper into narrow specialties, which we pursue almost in solitary confinement. This is particularly severe in the major research universities, but the same tendencies are there in growing degrees in all college faculties.

While academic departments must bear much of the responsibility for the institutionalization of such tendencies and their accompanying problems, departments are nevertheless also the most appropriate places to initiate the changes that must be made before the quality of college teaching can be improved significantly. It is in departments that the human resources of higher education are mobilized, and it is there that efforts to revitalize a sense of academic community can have the greatest success, since there already exists a base of shared values and interests on which to build. In our departments, we are likely already to possess much of what we need to know about good teaching—what it is, and how to do it—but that knowledge is now fragmented and locked in the isolated experiences of individual faculty members, unshared among colleagues who separately go about their common business.

The quality of teaching could be substantially improved simply through the sharing of ideas and experiences, especially among people working in the same field, but such a beneficial joining of forces is not likely to occur spontaneously. Here, the role of the department chairperson is crucial. Chairpersons must take the lead in bringing department members together in ways that enable them to comfortably discuss their own experiences and insights as teachers. Meetings—at least two or three a semester—are necessary. All department members should be expected to attend. Some may resent this demand on their time. Others may feel threatened by the issues, and initial meetings may amount to little more than gripe sessions, during which reluctant participants complain, perhaps bitterly, about the gross inadequacies of students and the unfair expectations of administrators. When the fury of the catharsis is spent, however, some matters of real substance can be addressed, if the chairperson persists and works hard between meetings, trying to convince individual colleagues that teaching excellence is a vital interest for the whole department. If everyone is made to feel that he or she has something of value to contribute to that common cause, then participation will in time be quite voluntary, discussions will be stimulating and constructive, and a sense of community will begin to develop.

In my own department, I have found that my colleagues, after overcoming some healthy skepticism, now seem to appreciate the opportunity to raise questions, receive advice, and contribute to the common good of our educational enterprise. In some of the early attempts to facilitate that process of sharing and cooperation—and, now, on a regular basis every semester—we simply gathered and distributed copies of everyone's course syllabi. A great deal of information is contained in those documents—information about literary and visual materials, field trips, and course assignments, as well as course goals and implied expectations for students. Most of us simply prepare those materials for our courses on our own, without any consultation, and we usually repeat what we have done before, which in many cases is similar to what was done to us as students. We seldom question the assumptions on which we structure our courses. It was not until after I became department chairperson and began routinely to receive and review copies of everyone's syllabi that I began to rethink some of the ways in which I taught my students. I learned much from my colleagues in this way and became convinced that the whole department would benefit from sharing such basic information. Furthermore, I soon discovered that this sharing process encouraged everyone to be much more thoughtful about course planning and the preparation of teaching materials. There is nothing like an audience of peers.

Building a greater sense of common purpose within a department or within a university is crucial, if we are to diminish the damage being inflicted on the educational environment by what Palmer (1987) has identified as "competitive individualism." Such competition "breeds silent, private combat for personal reward" (Palmer, 1987, p. 25), and it produces the envy and insecurity that make departmental politics so ugly and enervating. It also stifles the kind of open and honest critical discussion necessary for the improvement of teaching, because competitive individualism has a very strong tendency to make all criticism personal, something negative that is taken personally and that usually hurts and embitters people. Nevertheless, asserts Palmer (p. 25), there still remains a vital need for constructive disagreement and for the kind of "communal conflict of checking and correcting and enlarging the knowledge of individuals by drawing on the knowledge of the group," but such "healthy conflict is possible only in the context of supportive community."

Constructive criticism is an essential element of the department chairperson's stock in trade. The chairperson, like a player-coach, has to be fully familiar with the professional strengths and weaknesses of all department members, in order to know how to encourage their very best efforts as teacher-scholars. That requires, in turn, an ongoing process of professional evaluation.

In the University of Wisconsin system, such a process is mandated, since at least half of each year's salary increase must be based on merit. For the University of Wisconsin centers, where our primary mission is undergraduate liberal arts education, a very substantial portion of the annual review conducted by the chairperson and departmental executive committee deals with teaching. This provides a good opportunity for departments to discuss their teaching performance expectations, and the entire process produces a great deal of useful information about what is happening in our laboratories and lecture halls. Our experience may provide a useful example.

Each year, our department conducts student evaluations for all instructors and courses. Moreover, class observation reports are prepared by peers, and copies of every instructor's course materials, along with copies of everyone's recent publications and other scholarly work, are gathered. All of that is carefully considered during the formal evaluation exercise. Immediately following the committee's assessment of merit, the chairperson sends each department member a detailed report describing the entire department's accumulated accomplishments for the year, as well as what were found to be the primary achievements and deficiencies in each individual's own professional performance. The opening part is something of a departmental "state of the union" message, indicating the nature of the broader context in which each individual's work was perceived. In discussing the individual's work, the intention is that the tone be positive, complimentary, and personal. Recognition is given to the value of the individual contribution to the common cause, and appreciation is expressed for the skills and efforts that were required. When the message is critical, the comments are clear, constructive, and specific and are accompanied by recommendations for what can and ought to be done to bring about improvements or to compensate for weaknesses that cannot be overcome. Those recommendations invariably name specific department members who should be consulted for advice in making such changes. That, in turn, helps develop an internal network for mutual assistance, which strengthens the communal character of the department.

In this kind of evaluation, platitudes and generalities simply will not wash. The message is being sent to perceptive and sophisticated people, who can recognize bunk at a cursory glance. They resent insincere flattery and will be especially irritated with nitpicking and fault-finding innuendo. It is necessary to study the material with care and then hit the important issues head-on in precise language, saying what you mean and meaning what you say. Most faculty members will accept criticism aimed at their professional growth, especially if it is presented in a manner that recognizes their strengths and contributions.

To better foster teaching improvement, the department should at some point (early in its discussions) attempt to arrive at a consensus about the qualities and attitudes that it most wishes to encourage collectively. The thirty items in Figure 1 provide a good place to begin such a discussion. (If that list seems too long and cumbersome, you may wish to consider the seven principles for good practice in undergraduate education discussed in Chapter Three.) Both lists contain similar ideas, most of them discussed in the recent educational reform literature. Three points require special attention by department chairpersons in this consensus-building process.

At the very top of the Miami–Dade list (Figure 1) is the declaration that good teachers are "enthusiastic about their work." They are people who believe in the value of what they are doing and, even more than that, as Arrowsmith (1966, p. 56) pointed out, they are people with "gifts of the spirit . . . whose technique is not showmanship but a power of being." Bennett (1984, p. 16) makes the same point when he asserts that "good teachers cannot be dispassionate [but rather] are moved by the power of the works [they teach] and are able to convey that power to their students."

We can probably agree about the desirability of such intense involvement in both the substance and the process of teaching, but it must be appreciated, especially by department chairpersons, that such feelings are extremely difficult to sustain in isolation, when one is teaching courses semester after semester. We begin to hear echoes of our own lectures and forget which classes have already heard our best jokes. The support and understanding of an intellectually vital community that really loves learning, as well as the company of scholars who still experience a sense of joy from discussing books and ideas and have a shared mission, can be critical in preventing burnout and keeping alive

Figure 1. Miami–Dade's Characteristics of Excellence in Professors

As part of its teaching and learning project, a committee of professors and administrators at Miami–Dade Community College set out to identify the "core of fundamental characteristics" that define classroom excellence for a faculty member.

The list has yet to be approved formally, but so far committee members agree that excellent professors:

1. Are enthusiastic about their work.
2. Set challenging performance goals for themselves.
3. Set challenging performance goals for students.
4. Are committed to education as a profession.
5. Project a positive attitude about students' ability to learn.
6. Display behavior consistent with professional standards.
7. See students as individuals operating in a broader perspective beyond the classroom.
8. Treat students with respect.
9. Are available to students.
10. Listen attentively to what students say.
11. Are responsive to student needs.
12. Give corrective feedback promptly to students.
13. Are fair in their evaluations of student progress.
14. Present ideas clearly.
15. Respect diverse talents.
16. Create a climate conducive to learning.
17. Work collaboratively with colleagues.
18. Are knowledgeable about their work.
19. Integrate current subject matter into their work.
20. Provide perspectives that include a respect for diverse views.
21. Do their work in a well-prepared manner.
22. Do their work in a well-organized manner.
23. Are knowledgeable about how students learn.
24. Provide students with alternative ways of learning.
25. Stimulate intellectual curiosity.
26. Encourage independent thinking.
27. Provide cooperative learning opportunities for students.
28. Encourage students to be analytical listeners.
29. Give consideration to feedback from students and others.
30. Provide clear and substantial evidence that students have learned.

Source: The Chronicle of Higher Education, April 13, 1987, p. A13.

the zeal necessary for good teaching.

An enthusiasm for knowledge and for the sharing of knowledge is important, especially on the professor's side of the learning relationship, but "no factor seems to account for student learning and satisfaction with college more than faculty contact," according to Mortimer (1987, p. 40). In fact, Tinto (1988, p. 8), an expert on retention among college students, has also pointed out that "the frequency and perceived worth of interaction with faculty outside the classroom is the single strongest predictor of student voluntary departure." In spite of that, there are still large numbers of students who complain that no professor has taken any "special personal interest" in even their academic progress (Bennett, 1986, p. 29). Departments and department chairpersons have to work to rapidly and radically change this situation. Professors need to make contact—personal contact—with the individual men and women they are responsible for teaching. Our students need "to feel both the excitement and the responsibility that comes from joining a community of learning" (Boyer, 1987, p. 57).

Finally, for the good of students and professors alike, and for the sake of excellence in both learning and teaching, it is necessary to have what the Miami–Dade committee refers to as "challenging performance goals" (Figure 1). Expecting students to perform well becomes a self-fulfilling prophecy when teachers and institutions hold high expectations of themselves and make extra efforts. Expectations are something departments need to discuss, and an unwavering commitment must be made to goals that will challenge the entire learning community to grow.

In all of this, the department chairperson must take the lead, first through personal example, and work vigilantly to maintain a sense of common purpose concerning the department's teaching mission. Colleagues have to be encouraged, complimented, and criticized, without evoking either their envy or their anger, and an environment of mutual trust must be created. Unfortunately, many of the strongest currents of our culture and profession now push powerfully against such efforts. Although we may have a desire to belong to an intellectually vital, caring community (Boyer, 1987, p. 57), creating one is a terribly difficult work for which we are not well prepared, warns Palmer (1987, p. 20), whose own experience led him to conclude that "community is that place where the person you least want to live with lives."

The need to improve the quality of college teaching is urgent. For that to happen, we will have to care more deeply about learning and about one another and the intellectual growth of our students. Most of all, we will have to become more willing to move beyond self-interest and begin to understand better the realities of our dependence on each other (Boyer, 1987, p. 8). The very best hopes exist in academic departments, led by committed chairpersons.

References

Arrowsmith, W. "The Shamer of the Graduate Schools: A Plea for a New American Scholar." *Harper's Magazine,* March 1966, pp. 51–59.

Bennett, W. "To Reclaim a Legacy." *The Chronicle of Higher Education,* November 28, 1984, pp. 16–21.

Bennett, W. "Address Given at the Harvard University Three-Hundred-and-Fifty-Year Anniversary Celebration." *The Chronicle of Higher Education,* October 15, 1986, pp. 27–30.

Boyer, E. L. *College: The Undergraduate Experience in America.* New York: Harper & Row, 1987.

The Chronicle of Higher Education, April 13, 1987, p. A13.

Hamerow, T. S. *Reflections of History and Historians.* Madison: University of Wisconsin Press, 1987.

Handlin, O. *Truth in History.* Cambridge, Mass.: Harvard University Press, 1979.

Mortimer, K. "Involvement in Learning: Realizing the Potential of American Higher Education." *The Chronicle of Higher Education,* October 24, 1987, pp. 35–49.

Newman, F. *Higher Education and the American Resurgence.* Lawrenceville, N.J.: Princeton University Press, 1985.

Palmer, P. J. "Community, Conflict, and Ways of Knowing." *Change,* 1987, *19* (5), 20–26.

Tinto, V. "The Principles of Effective Retention." Unpublished paper presented at the University of Wisconsin Center Conference on College Student Retention, Marinette, Wisconsin, January 6, 1988.

Kerry A. Trask is an associate professor and chairperson of the University of Wisconsin Center's Department of History. His book In The Pursuit of Shadows *(Garland, in press) is a study of Massachusetts during the French and Indian War. He teaches courses in American history and western civilization, mostly at the introductory level.*

Index

J. H. McMillan, (ed.). *Assessing Students' Learning.*
New Directions for Teaching and Learning, no. 34. San Francisco, Jossey-Bass, Summer 1988.

ERRATUM

Page 62, lines 2-5:

This sentence should read: In this chapter, *experiential learning* is defined as learning in which the learner is in direct contact with the realities being studied or practiced to achieve a level of competence in a particular skill or knowledge domain.